# Poetry Explorers

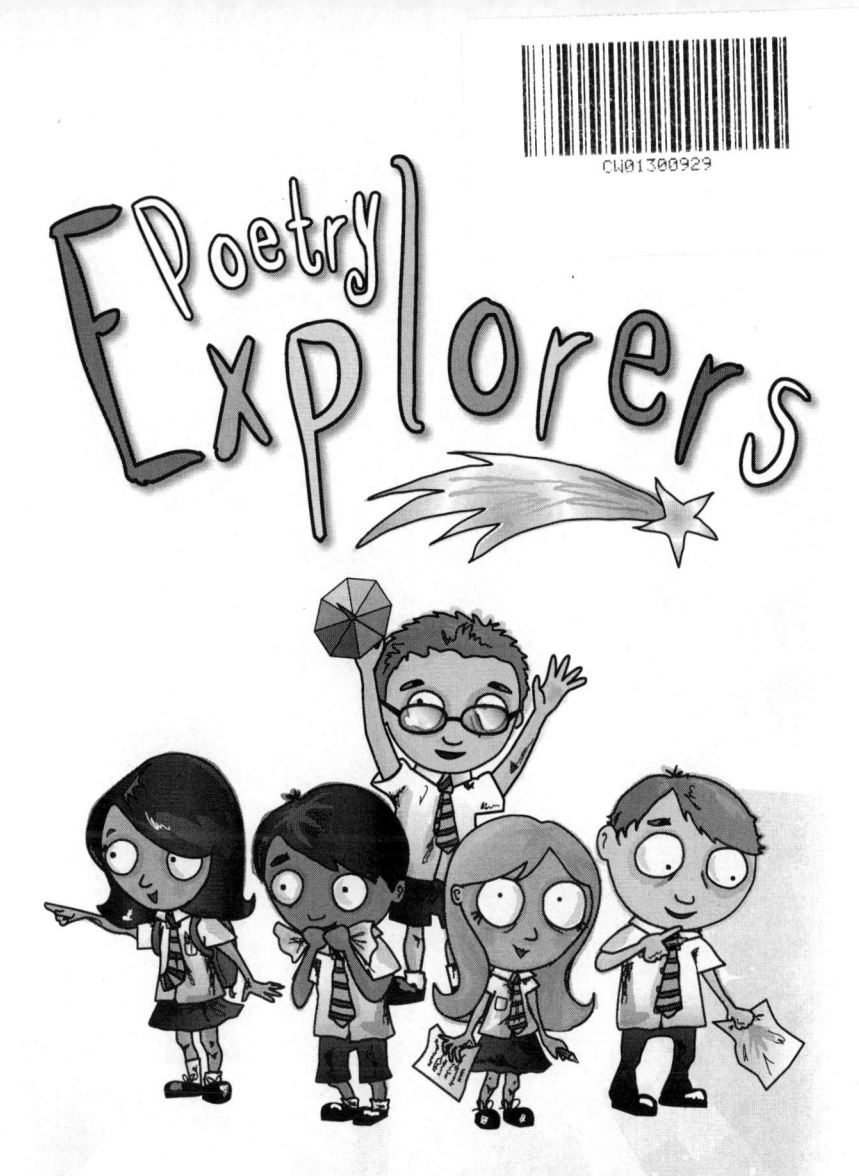

**West Yorkshire**

Edited by Claire Tupholme

First published in Great Britain in 2009 by

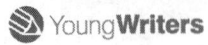

Young**Writers**

Remus House
Coltsfoot Drive
Peterborough
PE2 9JX
Telephone: 01733 890066
Website: www.youngwriters.co.uk

All Rights Reserved
Book Design by Spencer Hart
Illustrations by Ali Smith
© Copyright Contributors 2009
SB ISBN 978-1-84924-264-6

# Foreword

At Young Writers our defining aim is to promote an enjoyment of reading and writing amongst children and young adults. By giving aspiring poets the opportunity to see their work in print, their love of the written word as well as confidence in their own abilities has the chance to blossom.

Our latest competition Poetry Explorers was designed to introduce primary school children to the wonders of creative expression. They were given free reign to write on any theme and in any style, thus encouraging them to use and explore a variety of different poetic forms.

We are proud to present the resulting collection of regional anthologies which are an excellent showcase of young writing talent. With such a diverse range of entries received, the selection process was difficult yet very rewarding. From comical rhymes to poignant verses, there is plenty to entertain and inspire within these pages. We hope you agree that this collection bursting with imagination is one to treasure.

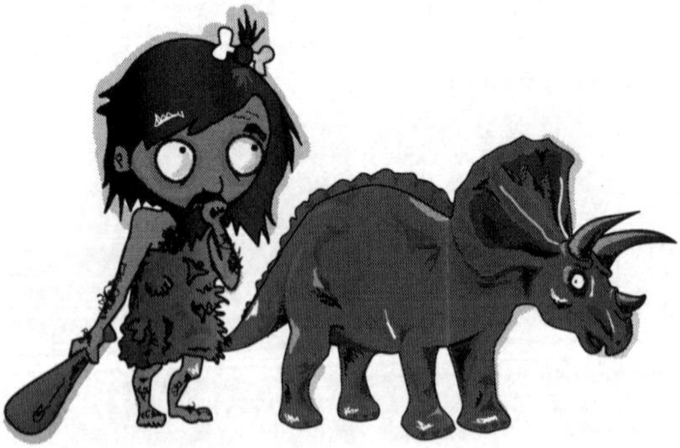

# Contents

## Allerton Primary School

| | |
|---|---|
| Aiysha Yaqub, Rameesha Mir & Rachel Conroy (10) | 1 |
| Lee Taylor & Matthew Gibson-Duxbury (10) | 1 |
| Ayisha Rafiq (10) & Zahra Ditta (11) | 2 |
| James Morfitt & Mustapha Ali (11) | 2 |
| Owen Li & Callum Hosty (10) | 3 |
| Bradley Russell (10) | 3 |
| Shannon Hopps (10) & Taiba Asghar (11) | 4 |
| Rebecca Caines & Bethany Miller (10) | 4 |
| Paris Ramsden-Hunt (10) & Debbie Michel (11) | 5 |
| Saffron Khan (10) | 5 |
| Aaron Kundi (10) | 6 |
| Maria Hussain (11) | 6 |

## Ashlands Primary School

| | |
|---|---|
| Rebekah Outterside (11) | 7 |
| 6GC Literacy Set | 8 |
| Daniel Lawton (11) | 9 |
| Michael Merrett (11) | 10 |
| Vikram Singh Uppal (11) | 11 |
| Mia Cooper (10) | 12 |
| Josh Ainge (10) | 12 |
| Niamh Dunne (10) | 13 |
| James DeMaine (10) | 13 |
| Tommy Matthews (10) | 14 |
| Nick Ducker (9) | 14 |
| Dudley Spence (10) | 15 |
| Edward Delves Martin (9) | 15 |
| James Webb (11) | 16 |

| | |
|---|---|
| Isla Lury (8) | 16 |
| Daniel Hayes (10) | 17 |
| Jasmine Jubb (8) | 17 |
| Jemima Spence (8) | 18 |
| Alex Barrett (9) | 18 |
| Oscar Slater (8) | 19 |
| Alastair Clarke (9) | 19 |
| Francesca Woodman (8) | 20 |
| Rachel Flint (9) | 20 |
| Ellie Mason (8) | 21 |
| Charlotte Simpson (8) | 21 |
| Toby Woodman (8) | 22 |
| Emma Jones (8) | 22 |
| Emily Martin (8) | 23 |
| Thomas Harris (8) | 23 |
| James McGowan (8) | 23 |
| Harry Hunt (8) | 24 |
| Oliver Wilson (8) | 24 |
| Robert Brear (10) | 24 |
| Chloe Slater (10) | 25 |
| Beth Galtry (10) | 25 |

## Carr Manor Primary School

| | |
|---|---|
| Shola Sewell (10) | 25 |
| Alexander Bald (11) | 26 |
| Hollie Belford (10) | 27 |
| Shanice Harumani (10) | 28 |
| Armani Anderson-Hamilton (10) | 29 |
| Charlotte Richardson (10) | 30 |
| Tonicha Allen (11) | 31 |
| Nicola Evans (11) | 32 |
| Rachel Horner (11) | 33 |
| Chloe Elmslie (10) | 34 |
| Rahul Sharma (11) | 35 |
| Eunice Ogedengbe (11) | 36 |
| Britney Rawlins (11) | 36 |
| Jaia Bharath (10) | 37 |

| | |
|---|---|
| Sumayyah Larabe Kiani (10) | 38 |
| Cara Bradshaw (11) | 39 |
| Makiel Hall (11) | 40 |
| Charlotte Barn (10) | 41 |

## England Lane J&I School

| | |
|---|---|
| Joshua Smith (9) | 41 |
| Maria Fairs (8) | 42 |
| Jack Scott-Ward (7), Jack Harvey & Ross Ellis (8) | 42 |
| Reece Brown (9) | 43 |
| Emily Egan (9) | 44 |
| Joe Winstanley (9) | 44 |
| Kieran Hoaksey (8) | 45 |
| Jordan Turner (7) & Bradley Stogden (8) | 45 |
| Louis Laverack (9) | 46 |
| Libby Shelton (9) | 46 |
| Ebony Ramskill, Jake Bottomley (7), Byron, Courtney & Connor (8) | 47 |
| Rhys Upton (8) | 47 |
| Callum Arckless (8) | 48 |
| Jayde Bradley (10) | 48 |

## Kippax Ash Tree Primary School

| | |
|---|---|
| Charlotte Bowler (9) | 49 |
| Olivia Rogers (9) | 50 |
| Dominic Peterson (10) | 51 |
| Steven Barrett (10) | 52 |
| Curtis Lee (9) | 53 |
| Kelsey Allaway (11) | 54 |
| Sophie Farrar (11) | 55 |
| Jake Kai Fox (9) | 56 |
| Molly Rose Harris (8) | 56 |
| Mollie Jo Wood (11) | 57 |
| Harry Pickersgill (8) | 57 |
| Bethany Ellis (9) | 58 |
| Brooke Smith (7) | 58 |
| Stephany Howson (8) | 59 |
| Liam Sidebottom (10) | 59 |
| Stuart Allcock (10) | 60 |
| Ellen Wright (9) | 60 |

| | |
|---|---|
| Jessica Gidman (10) | 61 |
| Kate Purchon (9) | 61 |
| Matthew Booth (11) | 62 |
| Matthew Handley (10) | 62 |
| Kelly Birkenshaw (10) | 63 |
| Emily Aveyard (10) | 63 |
| Carter Wilson (7) | 64 |
| Danielle Bentley (9) | 64 |
| Katie Knepper (10) | 65 |
| Bethany Jade England (11) | 65 |
| Charley Shepherd (9) | 66 |
| Kieran Haffenden (7) | 66 |
| Holly Doherty (8) | 67 |
| Emma Birtwhistle (8) | 67 |
| Kerry Richardson (10) | 68 |
| Katie Sanderson (10) | 68 |
| Rachael Birkenshaw (9) | 69 |
| Nicole Watson (11) | 69 |
| Russell Barton (10) | 70 |
| Sufian Thompson (8) | 70 |
| James Byers (11) | 71 |
| Maisie Louise Greer (8) | 71 |
| Jed Limbert (9) | 72 |
| Conor James Halkyard (10) | 72 |
| Connor Walls (7) | 73 |
| George Colledge (11) | 73 |
| Imogen Linley (8) | 74 |
| Christopher Thorp (11) | 74 |
| Leah Flintoft (11) | 75 |
| Jenna Burns (11) | 75 |
| Ben Hardcastle (10) | 76 |
| Lauren Obridge (11) | 76 |
| Ayesha Goggs (9) | 77 |
| Adam Hepworth (7) | 77 |
| Natalie Sterland (10) | 78 |
| Emily Brown (11) | 78 |
| Leah Bootland (7) | 79 |
| Oliver Thompson (10) | 79 |
| Emily Lunn (10) | 80 |
| Laura Georgia Wardell (11) | 80 |
| Sarah O'Neill (8) | 81 |
| Jake Crossland (10) | 81 |
| Rebecca Westerman (8) | 82 |

| | |
|---|---|
| Megan Laura Wright (11) | 82 |
| Jessica Snaddon (7) | 83 |
| Libby Latto (10) | 83 |
| Ellie Davis (8) | 84 |
| Ellie Doherty (8) | 84 |
| Lauren Morley (8) | 85 |
| Christopher Winter (10) | 85 |
| Joshua Whaley (10) | 86 |
| Kieron England (8) | 86 |
| Callum Grainger (10) | 87 |
| Jasmin Cartwright (7) | 87 |
| Georgia Cattle (9) | 88 |
| Sam Ward (11) | 88 |
| Aaron Booth (9) | 89 |
| Sam Lunn (7) | 89 |
| Hannah Obridge (8) | 89 |
| Nathan Newton (7) | 90 |
| Corrine Perkins (8) | 90 |
| Charlotte Byers (7) | 90 |
| Harry Goodall (7) | 91 |
| James Saxon (7) | 91 |

## Methodist J&I School

| | |
|---|---|
| Henry Milner (10) | 91 |
| Joseph Morris (10) | 92 |
| Sam Winder (10) | 93 |
| Jayne Davidson-Page (10) | 94 |
| Hannah Davidson-Page (10) | 94 |
| Michael Willis (10) | 95 |
| Grace Byrom (7) | 95 |
| Amy Winder (10) | 96 |
| Matthew Greener (10) | 96 |
| Lucy Cooper (10) | 97 |
| Olivia Marsh (8) | 97 |
| Antonia Stephenson (10) | 98 |
| Thomas Wolfe (10) | 99 |
| Ellis Abbott (10) | 99 |
| Elizabeth Arnott (10) | 100 |
| Joe Callaghan (10) | 100 |
| Marie Aylward (11) | 101 |
| Seth Jackson (10) | 101 |

| | |
|---|---|
| Daniel Thompson (9) | 102 |
| Abbey Matthews (7) | 102 |
| Victoria Truelove (9) | 103 |
| Ben Ascough (9) | 103 |
| Ismael Ajaz (11) | 104 |
| Emily Pittam (8) | 104 |
| Sam Thompson (9) | 105 |
| Alishah Arshid (10) | 105 |
| Megan Ball (10) | 106 |
| Nathan Hinley (10) | 106 |
| Owen Addy (10) | 107 |
| Aqeel Ajaz (9) | 107 |
| Samuel Atkinson (11) | 108 |
| Lucas John Blackwell (10) | 108 |

## Old Town Primary School

| | |
|---|---|
| Django Claughan (9) | 109 |
| Katy Blagg (11) | 110 |
| Joe Law (10) | 111 |
| Lugh Martin (10) | 112 |
| Molly Stansfield (10) | 113 |

## Primrose Lane Primary School

| | |
|---|---|
| Josh Mitchell (7) | 113 |
| Rachel Duxbury (8) | 114 |
| Alicia Batley (8) | 114 |
| Jemima Browning (8) | 115 |
| Lucy Toogood (7) | 115 |
| Ryan Lawn (8) | 116 |
| Sarah Kirsty Halliday (8) | 116 |
| Joseph Thomson (7) | 116 |
| Ben Spink (7) | 117 |
| Lily Dell (7) | 117 |
| Tom Hepworth (7) | 117 |
| James Cahill (7) | 118 |

## Richmond Hill Primary School

| | |
|---|---|
| Jasmine Simmons (7) | 118 |
| Alexander Tepsic (7) | 119 |
| Joe Daniels (7) | 119 |
| Ethan Wormald (8) | 119 |

## Towngate Primary School

Charlotte Rimmington (7) .................. 120
Matthew Wilson (8) ............................. 120
Amy Charlotte Pickering (7) ............... 121
Sophie Kay Jarman (8) ....................... 121
Molly Walker (7) .................................. 122
Harry Revell-Jackson (8) .................... 122
Zach Fletcher (7) ................................ 123
Ruth Sterry (7) .................................... 123
Nathan Brummitt (7) ........................... 123

## Wellington Primary School

Emma Street (10) ............................... 124
Joe Newell (9) ..................................... 124
Megan Spence-Hill (9) ........................ 125
Dominic Burdett (9) ............................ 125
Samir Cradock (8) .............................. 126
Hannah Scowby (8) ............................ 127
Morgan Dawson (8) ............................ 127
Nick Jasper (10) ................................. 128
Ashleigh Yates (8) .............................. 128
Asim Ali (10) ....................................... 129
Rahim Rashid (9) ................................ 129
Jessica Barron (10) ............................ 130
Adam Frost (10) ................................. 131
Aaron Kundi (10) ................................ 132
Nathanial Rhodes (11) ....................... 133
Nathan Crane (10) .............................. 134
David Stainsby (11) ............................ 135
James Smith (8) ................................. 136
Keiran Child (8) .................................. 136
Rosie Shackleton (10) ........................ 137
Thomas Rushworth (8) ....................... 137
Alicia Blum (10) .................................. 138
Lucy Tattersfield (7) ........................... 138
Rebecca Elyse Riley (9) ..................... 139

# The Poems

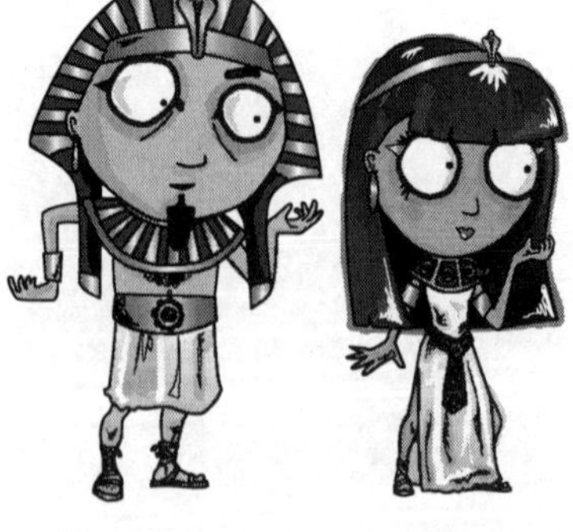

Poetry Explorers – West Yorkshire

# White Winter!

Snow is like a white-silver blanket
Covering the city.
She turns houses into palaces
With her magical touch
As she visits the earth below.

She knocks on our doors
Like she's desperate to enter.
She rattles our windows;
She is such an angry polar bear.

We won't let her in,
She will destroy our houses.
But to me she is a beautiful sight,
Like an angel from above.

Aiysha Yaqub, Rameesha Mir & Rachel Conroy (10)
**Allerton Primary School**

# Snow

Snow is like a beautiful white jacket,
All the kids want it.
The next day they run to get it,
But it has gone.
When you go to your friend's to play,
It is candyfloss and it sticks to your hair.
Some snow blows up when it hits the ground,
It sounds like gunfire.
*Boom! Bang!*

Lee Taylor & Matthew Gibson-Duxbury (10)
**Allerton Primary School**

# Rain!

Aggressive rain cautiously
Slides off hills
Like waterfalls pouring.
Anxious legs run to a dry place to dry off.

Light rain falls quietly
Onto the rooftops
Like dancing angels falling,
Making weak roofs leak, slowly and silently.

Angry rain falls loudly
Onto the playground
Like bouncing footballs falling,
Making the children stay inside, dry and warm.

Ayisha Rafiq (10) & Zahra Ditta (11)
**Allerton Primary School**

# Thunder

A thunderstorm is like a bang of fireworks,
It screams as it strikes down as fast as the wind;
Thunder is people shouting,
Thunder is like a tiger roaring,
When the sun comes out, thunder runs away;
But returns the next day, shrieking.
Thunder is pitch-black mist with lightning streaks.
Thunder is God moving furniture.
Thunder is a cheetah chasing its prey.
Thunder is like a panther growling.

James Morfitt & Mustapha Ali (11)
**Allerton Primary School**

# Rain

Aggressive rain slides off the hills
Like a waterfall on a cliffside.
Anxious legs quickly run for shelter
Away from the storm.

Soft rain falls quietly to the playground
Like a balloon lying on a mattress.
Loud tongues quietly catch refreshing
Drops of soft rain.

Angry hail bounces in the park
Like a child on a trampoline.
Busy hands quickly pack up picnics
Away from the angry hail.

Owen Li & Callum Hosty (10)
**Allerton Primary School**

# Rain

Rain drizzles down like a dripping tap.
He spits and drips to get us wet.
He can be sly at awkward times.
Rain is a damp, soggy sponge;
He is mischievous,
He runs down your back.
Clothes jump off the washing line,
When he begins to drip.
Umbrellas go up when he spits
And come down when he goes away.

Bradley Russell (10)
**Allerton Primary School**

# Winter Wonderland!

The beautiful Snow dances to the frosty ground,
While all the world is gracefully rotating around.
She touches your face, like a kiss on your forehead,
And your garden becomes a white blanket upon the city where
you live.

She races down the street quickly, spreading her arms,
Covering the street in a fluffy layer of thick cotton wool.
The Snow is feathers upon people's heads,
As all the excited children jump out of bed.

She brings smiles upon people's faces.
She spins, she twirls, on the roof she lands,
Joyfully creating a winter wonderland!

Shannon Hopps (10) & Taiba Asghar (11)
**Allerton Primary School**

# The Destructive Tornado

The monster silently rises,
A ballerina he is like.
He pivots on his tiptoes
As he spins ruinously down the lane,
Destroying all beauty and grace.
He dances shamefully down the misty street
Leaving chaos behind.
He wrecks everything in his path,
Rushing past like a bolt of lightning.
A ruined, silent city he abandons.

Rebecca Caines & Bethany Miller (10)
**Allerton Primary School**

## The Angry Storm

He enters the night with a
*Bang, crash, boom.*
He stomps around frowning at the moon.
He's furious and mean,
He's here to cause some damage.
His fangs are dripping,
He feels so savage.
He is manic, he is mad,
Like someone out of their mind.
He is always angry, never kind,
He is a raging bulldog.

Paris Ramsden-Hunt (10) & Debbie Michel (11)
**Allerton Primary School**

## Rain! Rain!

Tender Rain softly wets the sparkling garden.
She laughs mischievously as naughty children
Splash in small puddles,
Soaking their feet like a duck in a pond.

Urgent Rain quickly taps the window.
Children run out to play,
Wetting their heads like an umbrella.

Aggressive Rain rapidly falls to the ground.
Children run in to shelter,
Like a rabbit hiding from its predator.

Saffron Khan (10)
**Allerton Primary School**

# Rain

Clashing rainstorm
On the damp, ugly pavement,
Like a basketball.

Powerful, moody rain
Thrashing on the muddy field,
Mixing the mud into water.

Driving rainstorm
Spinning around in the windy air
Like a spinning tornado.

Aaron Kundi (10)
**Allerton Primary School**

# Rain!

Dribbling rain quietly twirls
Softly like a ballerina.
Children sleep in delight,
Silently catching refreshing raindrops.

The torrential rain clashes
Upon the buildings,
As the rain splashes down
And floods everything.

Maria Hussain (11)
**Allerton Primary School**

# It's Autumn

It's autumn, I'm back.
The golden-red, crunching leaves floating
Slowly to the ground.
The green grass saying goodbye,
And in its place, an army of remarkable colours.
The wind whipping across the streets,
Dashing round every corner,
Finding the leaves a new place to stay,
But never certain about the place.
Some nights are glorious,
Spectacular, stunning, bright colours
Suddenly blossoming into the sky.
The sun is going to rest,
Saying her final goodbyes
To the people she has warmed.
'Goodbye, my beautiful land,
I hope I have pleased you,
But now it is my time to go,'
She says, smiling sweetly.
'No! Please don't go,
We will lose all our beautiful leaves,'
The trees beg.
Children laughing, smiling,
Shivering in the autumn's chill,
Stuffing their faces with sugar,
As autumn tempts them with treats and goodies.
I'm autumn, and it's good to be back.

Rebekah Outterside (11)
**Ashlands Primary School**

# The Storm

As the sun wakes
It warms the rest of the sea,
It warms the people fishing
And children at their play.

But what sight does she see?
An oil spill from a tanker,
Plastic bags afloat in the water,
And drink cans tossed overboard.

The sun,
She sighs,
'Oh how can they treat my beautiful friend like this?
What has the sea ever done to them?'

And tears fall from the sun's eyes.
Clouds cover over so she can't see
The poor, dying, wasteland sea.

The wind whips up in anger,
The sea begins to churn,
The waves are building towers
Of angry waterfalls.

As the tankers rock about
They're oblivious to the stormy chaos,
But the smaller boats are tossed about,
Along with all the creatures.

One tiny boat calls up,
'Please Sun, calm the sea,
For all the small boats and animals
Have done no harm at all.'

Now the sun heard the little boats,
So she came out blazing, bright and hot.
The clouds all scattered from the heat
And again the sun warmed the restful sea.

And as the little boat sailed home
You could hear his fading voice,
'Thank you, beautiful Sun,
For calming down the storm.'

6GC Literacy Set
**Ashlands Primary School**

# The Autumn Tree And The Evergreen

The trees have leaves,
But not for long
As this autumn breeze
Will take them with ease.

'Oh, look at me,' said the autumn tree,
'With my lovely golden coat,
But look at the evergreen,
So horrid and green.'

'You won't be golden for long,'
Said the evergreen,
As the wind came rushing past.

'Oh no, no, no!' said the autumn tree,
'My golden leaves,
Come back to me.'
As he reached out, stretching for the leaves.

'Look who's laughing now,' said the evergreen.
'All your leaves are gone, now all you've got
Is brown, dry skin, while I still have a coat.'

Daniel Lawton (11)
**Ashlands Primary School**

# Autumn

My leaves are turning red and gold
And my conkers are falling down.
The children pick them up,
And on a little string they hang them
And swing them round and round.

They kick up the carpet of leaves
And down they fall again.
Red, gold, yellow and orange,
What beautiful colours they are.

Then come men, women and children,
With costumes galore and masks on faces,
All saying, 'Trick or treat?'
At the doors with golden pumpkins.

When the darkness comes,
The stars come out to twinkle.
As people start to gather,
The fire comes to life.
It dances to the bangs and booms
Of the blazing sky.

So that is autumn, lovely, yes,
But as it comes to die,
I must rest asleep
Under a blanket of cold white snow.

Michael Merrett (11)
**Ashlands Primary School**

# I Am Autumn

Now my time has come, I will prepare myself.
I will dress myself in red, yellow, gold and bronze,
I will put on my toffee apple earrings
And put on my pumpkin shoes.

I will wipe away all the wonderful colours
And leave them looking dull.
I will tell the conkers to fall,
I will call Jack Frost to bring some white,
And maybe a bit of chill.
He will cover every inch of the earth
From the ground to the top of a hill.

I will watch people snuggling up to a fire,
I will watch the children playing conkers
And playing trick or treat,
And families wrapping up warm.

I will make the night come quickly
And watch the fireworks.
I will make a bonfire burst up
And knit a blanket of mist.

I am Autumn.

Vikram Singh Uppal (11)
**Ashlands Primary School**

# When The Evergreen...

When the evergreen was settling to sleep
He heard a sob of sorrow.
'Oh Evergreen, how lucky you are to be
Green and beautiful, when I am dull!'
The conker tree cried.

The evergreen yawned, 'Consider yourself lucky,
Conker Tree, to have such colours, for you can go
From red to yellow, gold and maroon, even green,
In hats, shoes and magnificent capes!'

Conker Tree looked puzzled,
'But you are green and bright?
Your colours are like summer times.'
The evergreen sighed, 'But at Christmas,
People decorate trees!
The trees must be green and bright,
Therefore, the evergreen is perfect for that!'

He then wiped a tear from his eyes
And said with a sigh, 'Goodnight.'

Mia Cooper (10)
**Ashlands Primary School**

# Cereal — Haiku

Slowly pour the wet
Snow on the fluffy cushions
Of snap, crackle, pop.

Josh Ainge (10)
**Ashlands Primary School**

# My Sister ... The Leopard

The stairs creak as we sneak
Up to the lair of the leopard.
Frightened and trembling,
We approach the closed door.

I open it with fear,
Hoping that the leopard is not there.
Luckily she is not.
Her lair is tidy and neat,
But soon it's not
As we savage through the closed drawers.

Behind I feel her there looking,
Glaring at me.
I turn my head and in my fear
She pounces at me.
Nowhere to dodge or run,
My heart pounding hard.
I see my chance at the open door
And scramble to the safety of the hall.

Niamh Dunne (10)
**Ashlands Primary School**

# Cheese Toastie — Haiku

Crispy, crusty, hot
Warm-grilled, clamps heavenly crisp
With yellow oozing.

James DeMaine (10)
**Ashlands Primary School**

# Autumn Tree

I am a tree that has seen many an autumn.
I have seen my poor dying leaves as they have to go,
I have seen fireworks crackling in the sky,
I have seen children playing around in their costumes.

I am a tree that has felt many an autumn.
I have felt the pain of my leaves as they slowly drift to the ground,
I have felt the crack of fireworks as they go off,
I have felt the children's happiness as they get sweets at every door.

I am a tree that has heard many an autumn.
I have heard my leaves call for help as they fall to the ground,
I have heard huge cheers as huge fireworks explode,
I have heard the giggles of children as they scare people.

I am a tree that has seen many an autumn,
And will see many more.
I lose many leafy friends,
But more come back again.

Tommy Matthews (10)
**Ashlands Primary School**

# My Brother – Simile Poem

My brother is as crazy as a clown in a circus.
My brother is as funny as a comedian.
My brother is as cool as a punk on the street.
My brother has eyes as green as a traffic light glowing in the dark.
My brother is as noisy as a car horn.

Nick Ducker (9)
**Ashlands Primary School**

Poetry Explorers – West Yorkshire

# She's Changing

She's changing,
Gone is the beautiful emerald-green dress,
And in its place she wears
A fiery orange coat,
A scarf of gold leaves
And dancing firework shoes.

Looking down from the velvet evening sky,
The wind is perched on his favourite cushion,
He's jealous and annoyed with her vanity.

He dribbles on the clouds below,
Turning them black and grey.
He smiles as his shower turns on
And rains on the land.

Strong winds bellow and rip her skirt in two
And before she can say why,
She's naked, naked as a tree.

Dudley Spence (10)
**Ashlands Primary School**

# My Cat, Silky

My cat is as gentle as a feather rubbing on my leg.
My cat is as pretty as a pearl in the sea, gleaming in the sunlight.
My cat is as fast as lightning bolting from the sky.
My cat is so soft that he is like a piece of silk from the finest
                                                                  fabric shop.
My cat is as black as midnight with no twinkling stars in the sky.

Edward Delves Martin (9)
**Ashlands Primary School**

# Conker Tree

It's autumn now
And I've been growing conkers
All year round.
Now it's time for them to drop off.

Watching children play with them
Gives me a warm, sensational feeling.
Children wrapped up warm in hats and gloves,
Having the time of their life.

In the summer I feel lonely,
With nobody to watch and love.
No sparkly leaves to show off,
No squirrels or birds to play with.

I love watching fireworks bang and crackle,
A ray of colours bursting out.
Bonfires light up the dark, gloomy nights,
That's why I love autumn.

James Webb (11)
**Ashlands Primary School**

# My Dog

My dog is as cuddly as my favourite teddy.
My dog is as soft as new silk.
My dog's eyes are as brown as wood.
My dog is as black as the midnight sky.
My dog is as funny as a clown in a circus ring.
My dog is as gentle as a newborn kitten.

Isla Lury (8)
**Ashlands Primary School**

# My Tormenting Uncle, The Elephant Man

'Mine! *Mine!*' screeched Natasha and Jack,
Fighting over the last chocolate bar,
Not knowing their daddy, the elephant man,
Was trumpeting away, not so far.

'Mine! *Mine!*' they both wailed again
As the chocolate bar flew in the air.
Jack kicked Tash as the elephant walked in,
Giving both of them an evil glare.

*'You two! Go to your room!'*
He shoved them both into their beds.
'Hmm . . .' he said as he took the choc bar,
'I think *I* will eat this instead!'

*Chomp! Chomp!*

Daniel Hayes (10)
**Ashlands Primary School**

# My Dog, Bluebell

Bluebell is as fluffy as a cat.
Bluebell has one eye as blue as the sky.
Bluebell barks as loud as an aeroplane going by.
Bluebell is as cute as a gerbil.
Bluebell is as fast as a train going to London.

Jasmine Jubb (8)
**Ashlands Primary School**

# My Adorable Mum

My mum is warmer than a duvet
When you're cuddled up inside.
My mum is as clever as a dictionary
And an encyclopaedia put together.
My mum is as busy as a bee
Collecting pollen from the flowers.
My mum is as healthy as a lion
That runs around all day.
My mum is as friendly as a
Nurse talking to a patient.
My mum smells like perfume
That's just come out of the fridge.
My mum likes ginger tea
As much as a rhino likes mud.

Jemima Spence (8)
**Ashlands Primary School**

# My Sister

My sister shops like Victoria Beckham,
If she'd won the lottery.
My sister plays hockey like a champion.
My sister's eyes are as blue
As the calm summer's ocean.
My sister is as funny as a comedian
Juggling five lions and a hippopotamus.
My sister is as clever as a computer
That has been updated ninety times!

Alex Barrett (9)
**Ashlands Primary School**

## My Dog, Sunny

My dog is giddy as a mad kangaroo
Getting taken to the zoo.
My dog is as healthy as an
Olympic runner in the finals.
My dog is as pampered as the Queen
In bed getting served breakfast in her room!
My dog is as suspicious as
Sherlock Holmes solving a murder.
My dog is as loving as the bride
About to kiss the groom.
I will always love her
And she will love me!

Oscar Slater (8)
**Ashlands Primary School**

## My Goldfish Poem

My goldfish is as fast as a
Rocket going up into space.
My goldfish is as cheeky as a
Monkey playing hide-and-seek.
My goldfish is as cute as a
Baby penguin in your arms.
My goldfish is as small as a
Baby's chubby cheeks.
My goldfish is as shiny as
Gold with mirrors around it.

Alastair Clarke (9)
**Ashlands Primary School**

# My Mum

My mum cares as much as my grandma giving me a hug.
My mum's hair is as brown as a tree trunk
Stood in a beautiful garden.
My mum tries as much as a person on his driving test
And just about to finish.
My mum is as happy as Santa Claus delivering presents.
My mum is as helpful as Perfect Peter
Clearing out the classroom.
My mum is as lovely as a shopkeeper
Giving me a sweet for free.
My mum supports me as much as a
Coach training a football team.

Francesca Woodman (8)
**Ashlands Primary School**

# Truffle, The Rat

My rat is as brown as
a bear eating its tea.
My rat's nose is as wet as
the pavement on a stormy day.
My rat's as balanced as
a bat on a twig in the wind.
My rat is as cute as
a teddy snuggled in bed.
My rat is as quiet as
a mouse creeping past a sleeping cat.

Rachel Flint (9)
**Ashlands Primary School**

## My Hamster, Stitch

My hamster is as cute as a
Chimp swinging in the trees.
My hamster's eyes are as brown as
Chocolate that I eat from Thorntons.
My hamster is as fast as
Lightning striking through the air.
My hamster is as soft as
Silk, just like my new dress.
My hamster is as small as
An ant passing through the grass.
My hamster is as squeaky as
A whiteboard pen.

Ellie Mason (8)
**Ashlands Primary School**

## My Dog, Weston

My dog is as happy as a
Clown in the circus.
My dog is as soft as a silk bed.
My dog is as fast as lightning
When it hits the ground.
My dog is as noisy as an elephant
When an elephant's mad.
My dog is as cute as Pudsey Bear
When he smiles.

Charlotte Simpson (8)
**Ashlands Primary School**

# My Friend

My friend is as funny as a monkey
Swinging on a branch in the jungle.
My friend's eyes are as blue
As bluebells in a wood.
My friend's hair is as ginger
As a hamster in the sun.
My friend is as happy as a
Hippopotamus at a party.
My friend is as fast as
A cheetah in the wild.
My friend is as crazy
As a bull charging.

Toby Woodman (8)
**Ashlands Primary School**

# My Dad

My dad works as hard as a computer.
My dad is as strong as a gorilla.
My dad is as exciting as a juggler.
My dad has short hair like a Labrador.
My dad is as gentle as a kitten.

Emma Jones (8)
**Ashlands Primary School**

# My Dog, Poppy

My dog is as playful as a two-year-old toddler.
My dog is as happy as a monkey in a bath of bananas.
My dog runs like the wind.
My dog is as cute as a baby bear.
My dog is as small as a mouse.

Emily Martin (8)
**Ashlands Primary School**

# My Uncle

My uncle is as crafty as a fox.
My uncle is as tall as a train.
My uncle is as cool as a cucumber.
My uncle is as daft as a duck.
My uncle is as strong as a tank.

Thomas Harris (8)
**Ashlands Primary School**

# My Dog, Henry

My dog is as fast as an athlete winning a gold medal.
My dog is as gentle as my teddy bear.
My dog is like a horse eating some egg and sausages.
My dog is white and brown like a hamster in a cage.
My dog is as smart as a scientist in a lab.

James McGowan (8)
**Ashlands Primary School**

# My Sister

My sister is as sill as Harry Hill on 'TV Burp'.
My sister is as noisy as a radio turned up to full volume.
My sister is as funny as a clown at the circus.
My sister enjoys making things like an 'Art Attack' presenter.
My sister is as naughty as a bad-tempered cheetah at a busy zoo.

Harry Hunt (8)
**Ashlands Primary School**

# My Gerbil – Simile Poem

My gerbil is as soft as fluff in the washing machine.
My gerbil is as strong as a weight-lifting champion in the Olympics.
My gerbil is as fast as Usain Bolt in the Olympics.
My gerbil is as cute as Puss In Boots in 'Shrek'.
My gerbil is as chubby as a person on an unhealthy diet.

Oliver Wilson (8)
**Ashlands Primary School**

# Hula Hoops – Haiku

Crunchy heaven snack,
Rings from imagined weddings,
Great crispy delights.

Robert Brear (10)
**Ashlands Primary School**

## Rolo – Haiku

Solid milky shell,
Sensational golden glow,
Tongue tingling flavour.

### Chloe Slater (10)
**Ashlands Primary School**

## Cashew Nuts – Haiku

Salty, crunchy taste,
Rainbow shape, chestnut colour,
Smooth turning to sharp.

### Beth Galtry (10)
**Ashlands Primary School**

## Summer

My voice is the children,
My gaze is the sun's rays,
My smile is the flowers,
My breath is the fresh breeze,
My cloak is the cool shade,
All run and have fun,
I am the summer.

### Shola Sewell (10)
**Carr Manor Primary School**

# Dolphin! Dolphin!

Dolphin! Dolphin! King of the sea,
Playing with his friends with a lot of glee.
He hears a sound coming near,
All his friends shriek with fear.

Dolphin! Dolphin! All alone,
Does not know
What yet comes to him right now,
As a figure comes his way.

Dolphin! Dolphin! All goes black,
He soon awakes, as aliens stare.
He shrieks and cries but still no go,
As night falls, it all turns dark,
He still shrieks for his mum and dad.

Dolphin! Dolphin! Young and brave,
Used to be a worthy slave.
Now his spirit's dropped and gone,
And now he is the only one.

Dolphin! Dolphin! Bird of the sea,
Doing tricks for you and me.
Begging to stop as he's forced to do,
No hope, no time, as life goes on.

Dolphin! Dolphin! Going white!
Something's happening, no one knows.
He cries for someone to help,
But no one comes as he yelps and yelps.

Alexander Bald (11)
**Carr Manor Primary School**

# The Cheetah

Cheetah! Cheetah! Running fast,
The open space, so big, so vast.
The blazing sun beats down on his fur,
Whilst his loud motor purrs.

Cheetah! Cheetah! On the prowl,
Ready to pounce, ready to growl.
He lives a life so wild and free,
He gallops, he skips along with glee.

Cheetah! Cheetah! Up in a tree,
Watching gazelles and zebras run free.
He pounces, he falls to the ground,
He's got a buffalo, blood spreads around.

Cheetah! Cheetah! Dull and grey,
No more running, no more prey.
Oh how he wishes he could be free,
But now he's trapped in captivity.

Cheetah! Cheetah! Curled up on the floor,
He wants them to unlock his prison door.
The ready-made meat, all fatty and red,
Now everything's gone to his head.

Cheetah! Cheetah! Fading away,
He watches the night turn into day.
He's wilting away like the winter flowers,
There he sits for hours and hours.

Hollie Belford (10)
**Carr Manor Primary School**

# Zoos – Friend Or Foe?

Zoos, zoos can be cool,
Zoos, zoos can be cruel.
Ready meals every day,
But no one listens to what you say.

Tiger, tiger, about to expire,
In a cage, not to its desire.
No pounce here, no pounce there,
Living life saying it's not fair.

Dolphin, dolphin, having fun,
Swimming and splashing in the sun.
Swim, swim everywhere,
Entertaining bi-pods that stare.

Bear, bear says it's a dream,
But that's not what it may seem.
Can't roam here, can't roam there,
Because there's no space anywhere.

Penguin, penguin says life's good,
'Cause every day there's free food.
Waddle, waddle here, waddle, waddle there,
Leave the zoo? Wouldn't dare!

Zoos, zoos can be cool,
Zoos, zoos can be cruel.
Ready meals every day
But no one listens to what you say.

Shanice Harumani (10)
**Carr Manor Primary School**

# The Monkey Poem

Monkey, monkey swinging around
Never stops, never touches the ground,
Swings to trees in its sight,
Silent monkey at night.

Still in cage,
Old and alone.
Still so sad,
Lost colour, going pale.

Monkey, monkey in a cage,
Now can't swing, filled with rage,
Dreaming what once used to be,
Now held in captivity.

Still in cage,
Old and alone.
Still so sad,
Lost colour, going pale.

Now in cage, power gone,
Pacing, pacing, on and on.
Now day goes by very slow,
Now he feels very low.

Still in cage,
Old and alone.
Still so sad,
Lost colour, going pale.

Armani Anderson-Hamilton (10)
**Carr Manor Primary School**

# Lion! Lion!

Lion! Lion! Enjoying your day,
Hunting around for your prey.
Charging left and charging right,
You sleep in the rain all through the night.

Lion! Lion! Full of fear,
Too many kids, they get too near.
Three paces left and three paces right,
Can barely even see the light.

Lion! Lion! Turning grey,
No more energy left to play.
You just feel like you're in Hell,
Trapped in your tiny prison cell.

Lion! Lion! Humiliated, sad,
This torture is turning you ever so bad.
There in prison you will lay,
You really don't want to stay.

Lion! Lion! Lack of power,
Will you last another hour?
You can smell the fumes of cars
Through your tiny prison bars.

Charlotte Richardson (10)
**Carr Manor Primary School**

# Lion! Lion!

Lion! Lion! Upon your throne,
In a cage sat all alone.
Pacing up and down your cell,
Feeling like you're in Hell.

Lion! Lion! Freezing cold,
Alone, sick and turning old.
Everyone could hear your growl,
Now you can barely leap and prowl.

Lion! Lion! In the past,
Thundering on so proud and fast.
You can only smell the fumes of cars,
Through your cold, dreary prison bars.

Lion! Lion! Turning grey,
No more hunting for your prey.
You're so weak, you're on the ground,
No more energy left to pound.

Lion! Lion! Humiliated and sad,
Rocking shows you're going mad.
You can only hear a dreadful sound
Of horrible cars zooming around.

Tonicha Allen (11)
**Carr Manor Primary School**

# Lion! Lion!

Lion! Lion! Packed up with fear
In a cage with people too near.
He paces around all day and night,
Knowing that he's lost his rights.

Lion! Lion! Freezing cold,
Tired, sick and growing old.
Hiding away from the light,
Full with anger and with fright.

Lion! Lion! Dreaming of the past,
Of wide open plains that are so vast.
However, now in reality,
He is in captivity.

Lion! Lion! No more bite,
Lacking some confidence and some might,
So humiliated and ever so sad,
His rocking shows he's going mad.

Lion! Lion! Is it true
That we could be so cruel to you?
You sit and pretend to be so proud,
Just for all the gawking crowds.

Nicola Evans (11)
**Carr Manor Primary School**

# Poetry Explorers – West Yorkshire

# Tiger!

Tiger! Tiger! Bold and bright!
Stands out for miles in the night.
He roars, he pounces, he kills for blood,
So savage and ruthless . . .
Never heard of mercy.

Tiger! Tiger! Fiery fur!
Rage burns in his eyes forever.
For food he kills, mostly for fun,
So silent and sneaky, yet ever so deadly,
Never heard of peace.

Tiger! Tiger! He roars so loud!
Respected by all that breathe.
He sprints and pounces on his prey,
Sleeps all night, kills all day,
Never heard of happiness.

Tiger! Tiger! Beautiful and fiery!
Yet at one little noise, he wants to chase,
To kill, to taste blood, to take a life,
To fill his belly yet again.
Never heard of love.

Rachel Horner (11)
**Carr Manor Primary School**

# Lion, Lion

Lion, lion, golden no more,
In a cage twice his height.
Seven paces left, seven paces right,
So now the lion's lost all his might.

Lion, lion, used to be king,
In a cage with no bling, bling!
He just strolls to and fro,
Now no longer with his bro!

Lion, lion, strong and brave,
Once lived in a cave.
Now he can't kill his lunch
Because he's left his useful bunch.

Lion, lion, freezing cold,
Sick, tired, growing old.
No joy, no space, no prey,
Now he's old and grey.

Lion, lion, once gold,
Now is wet and getting cold.
In his cage, he slowly fades away.

Chloe Elmslie (10)
**Carr Manor Primary School**

# My Grandad Is An Angel From Heaven

My grandad is an angel from Heaven,
Who lived a grand life till eighty-seven.
My maths is a little bad,
As he is not here to help, that is sad.

Now to prove all his deeds are tall.
He leaves his wife and us all,
A gap of sorrow he does leave.

With his sweet memories
Which we will seal.
An angel from Heaven is not heard.

A little time with him I spent,
He was my pillar of strength,
Who I will like to remember
As an angel from Heaven.

Now he is back with God,
To shine as a little star,
Who will always watch over me
From the sky above.

Rahul Sharma (11)
**Carr Manor Primary School**

# Yes!

A smile says yes,
A frown says no.
When a cheetah says fast,
A turtle says slow.

A footballer says kick,
A swimmer says dive.
A reporter says here,
The news says live.

A centipede says crawl,
A bee says pest.
When the clouds say rain,
The sun says rest.

A baby says play,
A mother says stress.
A fashion designer says new,
A model says dress.

Eunice Ogedengbe (11)
**Carr Manor Primary School**

# My Sister

My sister is the queen of drama,
She gets everything her way.
My mum is her favourite armour,
She annoys me every day.
I once tired to stop her
And now I am a defenceless sister!

Britney Rawlins (11)
**Carr Manor Primary School**

*Poetry Explorers – West Yorkshire*

# Turtle! Turtle!

Turtle! Turtle! Slow and paced,
Never gets to win the race.
Now his time's come and gone,
He was left and is the only one.

Turtle! Turtle! Fury of the sea,
By the ocean or next to a tree.
Once living in the deep blue,
Now next door to a kangaroo.

Turtle! Turtle! In his shell,
Nobody knows if he's unwell.
Tired of his life's misery,
Because he's so lonely.

Turtle! Turtle! Going grey,
Used to laugh and play all day.
People always come too near,
So he shrieks in more fear.

Jaia Bharath (10)
**Carr Manor Primary School**

# Lion, Lion

Lion, lion, once felt like a king,
In a cage so dull and dim.
He moved like a cheetah fast,
He felt so sad he lost his will.

Lion, lion, now speedy and strong,
In a cage singing a lonely song.
He moved like dead prey,
So he had a minute to think of the day.

Lion, lion, locked up and thin,
He pounced like the scary, roaring wind.
He used to make the noise of a slammed door,
Now he has a tiny roar.

Lion, lion, staring from his cage,
Sadly, playing with no mates.
No killing meals of animals.
There he sits, day by day.

Sumayyah Larabe Kiani (10)
**Carr Manor Primary School**

# Bear

Bear! Bear! Soft and brown,
In the woods strolling around.
He leisurely roams through the trees,
Enjoying life, being free.

Bear! Bear! Tatty and sore,
In a circus entertaining more.
He dances along with misery,
Thinking of where he needs to be.

Bear! Bear! Beaten and poked,
In a cage lost, no hope,
He takes four paces but no more,
Then he soon collapses to the floor.

Bear! Bear! Soft and brown,
Back in the woods where he was found.
He leisurely roams back through the trees,
Wondering why he's back and free.

Cara Bradshaw (11)
**Carr Manor Primary School**

# Lion

Lion, lion shining bright,
Even in the dead of night.
Lion, lion, once roaming free,
Now trapped in captivity.

Lion, lion finishing his meat,
Chasing for a kill on his feet.
Sinks his claws into his kill,
Eats it all to get his fill.

Lion colour fading away,
In a cage, no longer able to play.
All cramped up and all hope lost,
The lion is no longer the boss.

Makiel Hall (11)
**Carr Manor Primary School**

# Elephant

Elephant! Elephant! Strolling free,
In the wild, quiet and grassy,
She roams around with her baby calf,
Wrapping her trunk round like a scarf.

Elephant! Elephant! Broken and sad,
In the wild leaving the life she had,
She collapses next to her baby child,
The ends of her tusks carried into the wild.

Elephant! Elephant! Lifts up slowly,
Looks up and sees her baby, lonely,
On top of her mother the baby lays,
With a cute little smile upon her face.

Charlotte Barn (10)
**Carr Manor Primary School**

# My Dreams

M ake a goal, the time is now
Y ou can ask for help if you wish

D isappointed when not achieved
R ising to the top
E stablish your goal
A ccomplish your target
M ake the most of your time
S eek for success.

Joshua Smith (9)
**England Lane J&I School**

# Going For Your Dream

G oing for your dreams
O ver all you can achieve
I n your own time you will get there
N ever give up
G reat award

F or you
O pen up the world
R each your dream

Y ou can get there
O ver all you can reach your dream
U p you can go
R each for the stars

D on't give up your dream
R each the finish line
E nter the world
A dream is hard to break
M ake sure you try your best.

Maria Fairs (8)
**England Lane J&I School**

# My Hand Reaches For Victory

My hand reaches for victory.
My hand waves hello to you.
My hand grasps as it moves.
My hand helps you climb a wall.
My hand shakes goodbye.

Jack Scott-Ward (7), Jack Harvey & Ross Ellis (8)
**England Lane J&I School**

# Believe In Yourself

B elieve you can do it
E nter your imagination
L ink into your heart
I n your heart is pumping mad
E nter your soul
V ary your strong dreams
E ncourage yourself

I nspired to succeed
N ever give up

Y ou'll reach your goal
O pen your heart
U nderstand you will have to work hard
R eveal your heart's desire
S mell your victory
E ncourage yourself to do it
L et yourself do it
F antasy will come!

Reece Brown (9)
**England Lane J&I School**

# Reach For The Stars

R each for the stars
E very step you take is worth it
A lways try and never give up
C ome on, keep on going!
H elp is there if you need it.

F ollow your dreams
O vercome your fears
R un faster and faster, you'll get there in the end

T ake your time, get it right
H ear your dreams, they're calling out for you
E ven if you fall I know you'll get back up

S oon you will reach your goal
T here's always hope
A chieve your goal, you're nearly there
R each for your target
S uccess!

Emily Egan (9)
**England Lane J&I School**

# Effort

E very step and you will get closer
F aster and faster you will get to your goal
F ollow your dream
O vercome your fears
R eally try your best
T he end for you is success.

Joe Winstanley (9)
**England Lane J&I School**

# Going For Goals

G leaming stars in the sky
O pening your dreams
I 'll try my very best
N obody will stop me
G o for your goal and never stop believing

F eel free and go with your heart's desire
O pen your imagination
R each for the stars

G oals are hard to reach
O vercome people that stand in your way
A ll has to be fair
L earn new skills
S uccess.

Kieran Hoaksey (8)
**England Lane J&I School**

# My Hand And Me

My hand grasps my pencil.
My hand waves goodbye.
My hand pulls you tightly.
My hand feels pleasure.
My hand holds others.
My hand gives gifts.
My hand shakes with nerves.
My hand takes toys.

Jordan Turner (7) & Bradley Stogden (8)
**England Lane J&I School**

# Going For Goals

G oing for goals is important for all
O pening your imagination
I deally goals would be easily achieved
N earer you step towards your goals
G oals are hard to be fulfilled

F eel free to get a goal
O ften you have to work hard
R each for the stars

G et your goal completed
O vercome your fears
A chieve your goals
L earn new skills
S oon you will reach your dream.

Louis Laverack (9)
**England Lane J&I School**

# Success

S uccess can move you further
U se your skills, you'll get better
C ompete in a race
C ontrol your mind to concentrate
E veryone will be proud of you
S ome things are not easy
S mile when you reach your goal.

Libby Shelton (9)
**England Lane J&I School**

## Our Head Teacher's Cupboard

Our head teacher has a cupboard,
It must be magic because
It has stickers for very good children,
Hard work for naughty ones,
Pens, pencils, paper and a pencil case.
A mobile phone for emergencies,
A rubber for mistakes,
Letters to send home to our parents,
A laptop to keep her busy,
And the most important thing in her cupboard,
*Chocolate!* It's bad for her teeth,
But she doesn't care!

Ebony Ramskill, Jake Bottomley (7), Byron, Courtney & Connor (8)
**England Lane J&I School**

## Effort

E veryone should try hard
F or your goal
F ollow your dream
O ften you think it is easy, but it is not
R eally be determined, never give up
T ry your best.

Rhys Upton (8)
**England Lane J&I School**

# Wishes

W ishes are things in your head
I t could be your dream to realise
S o work hard and reach your goal
H elpful people can help you achieve success
E veryone can try their best
S coring goals is a challenge.

**Callum Arckless (8)**
**England Lane J&I School**

# Effort

E nter to your greatest dreams
F aster and faster you will go and achieve your goal
F ollow your path to your goal
O vercome your fears
R each for the stars
T ry your hardest to succeed.

**Jayde Bradley (10)**
**England Lane J&I School**

# Winter – Haikus

I do not like slush
I think it is amazing
The snow is fluffy.

It is fluffy snow
It is also dangerous
It is very smooth.

It is so icy
Robins are flying about
It is so funny.

Children are playing
Throwing snowballs everywhere
Bright, sparkling snowballs.

Opening presents
Children jumping out of bed
Thanking everyone.

Snowflakes drifting down
Lots of different shaped snowflakes
The snow is settling.

Presents coming soon
Presents arriving in town
Getting excited.

I do not like slush
I think it is amazing
The snow is fluffy.

Charlotte Bowler (9)
**Kippax Ash Tree Primary School**

# Winter – Haikus

The sharp glassy ice
The wintery wonderland
It falls from the sky.

The glimmering snow
Glistening brightly at you
Shining in your eyes.

Frosty snowflakes come
They come gliding down on you
They leave lumpy snow.

People in the snow
Making enormous snowmen
And sledding down hills.

Christmas trees ready
With people decorating
Stockings up on walls.

The icy snowflakes
Floating down on your doorstep
Landing with a crack.

Presents arriving
With lots of bows and wrapping
Onto your doorstep.

Olivia Rogers (9)
**Kippax Ash Tree Primary School**

Poetry Explorers – West Yorkshire

# Tidy Bedroom!

One dreadful day in May,
I was forced to tidy my bedroom,
But all I wanted to do was play,
Especially with my favourite game called 'Doctor Fume'.

I crawled into my room
And stared around with terror.
It looked like the world's messiest tomb,
So I shouted down to Dad, 'This is horror!'

When I finally started tidying,
I found games like 'Find The Mice Grinding'
And bits of food like raw banana,
And an excellent film called 'Futurama'.

I was at it for six hours,
By now I was falling down like towers.
I was only halfway through,
When Dad shouted, 'Don't forget the Hoover too!'

When I had finally finished, I got a sheet
And carefully hung it from my bed to my feet.
I looked at it cheerfully, I had even made a den.
My sister said, 'Ten out of ten!'

Dominic Peterson (10)
**Kippax Ash Tree Primary School**

# Water Breathing

If I could breathe water
I would swim through the coral cities,
Gazing at the beautiful fish.

If I could breathe water,
I would surf the glistening waves
As they carry across the vast sea.

If I could breathe water
I would venture to the very bottom of the ocean
Where the monsters of the deep lurk in the dark.

If I could breathe water
I would listen to the overwhelming shout of the shark,
Making sure he didn't see me.

If I could breathe water
I would smell the dead prey of the piranhas,
Glad they didn't get me.

If I could breathe water I would
Gaze at the silver mountains,
Wishing I could climb them.

Steven Barrett (10)
**Kippax Ash Tree Primary School**

## Flying Car

If I had a flying car I would
Stare at the spacemen in their
Shiny white suits floating around.

If I had a flying car I would
Zoom up to the beautiful white clouds
And float in the middle of them.

If I had a flying car I would
Go up and fly with a bundle of blackbirds
And watch them swoop down.

If I had a flying car I would
Accelerate up beside a plane
And wave to all the giddy, excited passengers.

If I had a flying car I would
Go up to space and look
At all the colourful planets.

If I had a flying car I would
Dream of going all the way to Pluto
And go on the freezing cold planet.

Curtis Lee (9)
**Kippax Ash Tree Primary School**

# Walking Through The Woods

Looking at the wood's path
Wishing I was doing maths
Wondering if I should go home
By myself, all alone?
As I go in I hear a howl
That was definitely not an owl
Maybe a wolf or a fox?
I want to be in a box
*Click*, I hear from behind
Don't turn, just be kind
Help, there's a rat
Oh my goodness, a bat
There's a shadow with a shocking face
Why can't I be in a different place?
Almost at the end
It is just around the bend
Oh my goodness, a deer
Why, why, why am I here?
I've got a sour tum
But finally I'm with Mum.

Kelsey Allaway (11)
**Kippax Ash Tree Primary School**

# I Didn't Hand My Homework In

I didn't hand my homework in,
My father threw it in the bin.
I went to the shops to buy some hay,
To think about what I could say.

I could say my dog had chewed it up
And put it in a china cup,
But all my friends would tell on me
And I'd go to bed without my tea.

Or if I'm lucky I could say
A gust of wind had blown it away,
But of course the weather was sunny and light
And that excuse didn't seem very bright.

I thought and thought most of the day
Of what I could and couldn't say.
I've learnt that I should do my work,
So I don't turn out a total jerk.

I'll leave school and do so well,
But I've always got this tale to tell.

Sophie Farrar (11)
**Kippax Ash Tree Primary School**

# If I Was A Tiger

If I was a tiger
I would take over the jungle
Like a fierce predator.

If I was a tiger
I would have black and orange stripes
And be camouflaged in the green and long grass.

If I was a tiger
I would sneak around the green grass
In the jungle and pounce on my prey.

If I was a tiger
I would hunt for meat to eat.

If I was a tiger
I would defend the other tigers
And kill my prey.

If I was a tiger
My stripes would be bright as the sun.

Tigers are predators, hunters, fierce, furious killers.

Jake Kai Fox (9)
**Kippax Ash Tree Primary School**

# Friends

Me and my friend have fun
Me and my friend explore
We leap, we skip and we run
There's an adventure we cannot ignore.

Molly Rose Harris (8)
**Kippax Ash Tree Primary School**

# The Street

Walking down the street
With a slow and steady beat
I can feel the heat
Growing on my feet
I hear whistling winds
Through towering trees
As I walk
I'm being stalked
I turn around
There is no sound
I see winding paths
That disappear in mysterious mist
I see a black cat
Chasing a bat
I hear eerie creaks
From the demon following me
When will this street end?
It's just around the bend
I am relieved . . .

Mollie Jo Wood (11)
**Kippax Ash Tree Primary School**

# Christmas

Snow is glistening on the ground,
Santa's footprints have been found,
Turkey and mince pies, lovely food to eat,
Lots of lovely presents, oh what a treat.

Harry Pickersgill (8)
**Kippax Ash Tree Primary School**

# Super Powers

If I had super powers
I would save the world from evil villains.

If I had super powers
I would zoom past buildings as fast as a roaring engine.

If I had super powers
I would guard the people and keep them safe.

If I had super powers
I would fly up to space and keep aliens far away.

If I had super powers
I would watch over from up above.

If I had super powers
I would stay by everyone's side forever.

If I had super powers
I would dream of being famous.

If I had super powers
I would keep everything perfect and the same.

Bethany Ellis (9)
**Kippax Ash Tree Primary School**

# School Daze

I like going to school, it can be cool,
Especially when boys and girls play the fool,
But learning can be a pain,
Sometimes it's hard to train my brain.

Brooke Smith (7)
**Kippax Ash Tree Primary School**

# Snowfall

Snow is bright
All fluffy and white
Falls day and night
From frozen rain
Melts away down the drain.

Snow falls all around
Making no sound
It crushes under feet
Laying in all the streets.

Snow is ice-cold
To make snowmen with hat of old
Coal eyes and carrots for noses
I need wrapping up in lovely warm clothes.

Snow is fun to play in the sun
But can be dangerous to other road users
So keep this to hand
Wrap up warm and keep safety in mind at all times.

Stephany Howson (8)
**Kippax Ash Tree Primary School**

# Liam's Poem

L iam Sidebottom
I support Liverpool Football Club
A Learning Log is really fun
M y Learning Log is really fun
S now is really fun to play with.

Liam Sidebottom (10)
**Kippax Ash Tree Primary School**

# If I Could Transform

If I could transform
I would transform into a giant fish
And swim round the world with a shark.

If I could transform
I would transform into a monkey
And swing along the trees smoothly.

If I could transform
I would transform into a cheetah
And run like the wind.

If I could transform
I would transform into a giraffe
And touch the fluffy clouds.

If I could transform
I would transform into a bird
And zoom to space like a spaceship.

Stuart Allcock (10)
**Kippax Ash Tree Primary School**

# The Bird – Haikus

The bird likes to sit
In his very hollow tree
Where he has his tea.

The bird knows his way
With his eagle-eye vision
He can see it all.

Ellen Wright (9)
**Kippax Ash Tree Primary School**

# Flying Powers

If I had flying powers
I would whizz up to the moon
And touch the tip of the moon sparkling.

If I had flying powers
I would fly as fast as the whistling wind
And get blown away to another country.

If I had flying powers
I would sing sweetly as the sun was rising up
And sing as soft as an opera singer.

If I had flying powers
I would fly like a magic carpet
Slowly dancing up and down to the sound of music.

If I had flying powers
I would fly to the cotton wool clouds
And gaze at the world from above.

Jessica Gidman (10)
**Kippax Ash Tree Primary School**

# The Birds In The Garden

The birds in the garden chirp and tweet
The birds in the garden eat and sleep
The birds in the garden peck and drink
The birds in the garden wash and think
The birds in the garden, big and small
The birds in the garden, I love them all.

Kate Purchon (9)
**Kippax Ash Tree Primary School**

# Late

Got my breakfast
Cereal rattled, 'Please pour me out!'
'Can't,' I said, 'late.'

Got in the car
Engine revved, 'Start me up.'
'Can't,' I said, 'late.'

Driving the car
Horn beeped, 'Hurry up.'
'Can't,' I said, 'late.'

Got to work
Machine rumbled, 'Work on me.'
'Can't,' I said, 'late.'

Went for dinner
Sandwich growled, 'Eat me up.'
'Can't,' I said, late!'

**Matthew Booth (11)**
Kippax Ash Tree Primary School

# Winter

W inter like a blanket of snow
I n the snow you play
N ew season, it's winter, it is snowing
T rousers wet and cold because of the snow
E nd of summer, now in winter
R eally cold, really wet, really white.

**Matthew Handley (10)**
Kippax Ash Tree Primary School

# A Loving Friend

One day I shall,
Shall find a man,
That man who kissed my lips,
But if he shall fail,
Fail shall let me fall
And in those arms,
Those gentle arms,
The arms of my friends,

My friends, the ones that I trust,
I trust through my heart,
My heart which was burned by him.
My heart which was saved by her,
The her who I call friend,
The him who I once called love,
But when they break my heart,
It shall heal with a friend.

Kelly Birkenshaw (10)
**Kippax Ash Tree Primary School**

# The Hippo

H ungry hippo lies in the sun
I n the mud having fun
P utting her hip-hop all into place
P lacing her belly into the lake
O pening her mouth, having a yawn
   while she sits there all forlorn.

Emily Aveyard (10)
**Kippax Ash Tree Primary School**

# Racing Cars

Racing cars are shiny,
They make a lot of noise,
I don't have a real one,
But I have some that are toys.
Some have big black tyres,
Some have stickers too,
Some have big red spoilers,
But I've only seen a few.
When I get older
I want a big race car
And a shiny helmet,
So I can drive it far.
But my favourite thing of all
Is the *vrooming* engine sound,
And seeing them on the circuit
Going round and round and round.

Carter Wilson (7)
**Kippax Ash Tree Primary School**

# Undersea

I can see the fish of many colours,
Swishing by, trying to get away
From the big white shark.
The shark has gone, now the fish are back.
As bubbles rise from my mouth,
I pounce out of the water
Into the sunlight and past the stars.

Danielle Bentley (9)
**Kippax Ash Tree Primary School**

# Ash Tree – Acrostic

A n achieving school like Kippax Ash Tree Primary is
S afe and successful
H appy and has good ideas

T ruthful and uses teamwork skills
R espectful and resourceful
E nergetic and sporty
E nthusiastic and helpful

P olite and friendly
R eliable and caring
I ndependent and interesting
M arvellous and delightful
A ctive and healthy
R esponsible and joyful
Y ou should come to Kippax Ash Tree!

Katie Knepper (10)
**Kippax Ash Tree Primary School**

# Sunshine

S un shining bright and yellow
U nder the sand we buried our dad
N ever want to go home
S pades and buckets on the beach
H ot sand between your toes
I ce cream topped with chocolate
N ever-ending fun
E xciting things to see and do.

Bethany Jade England (11)
**Kippax Ash Tree Primary School**

# Winter's Day

As I look outside
I can see the glistening snow shining up at me.

As I look outside
The snow is like a blanket all over the floor.

As I look outside
Slippery ice everywhere, ages till it melts.

As I look outside
People gathering snow clumps to make some snowmen.

As I look outside
People collecting snow chunks to throw at people.

As I look outside
In seven days time it will all have gone.

Charley Shepherd (9)
**Kippax Ash Tree Primary School**

# Bullies

I don't like bullies, they make me mad
They pick on people and make them sad
That's not very nice and I don't know why
They call people names and make them cry.

So if you don't like what they do
It's time to teach them a thing or two
Don't get even and don't get mad
Go tell your teacher or your mum or dad.

Kieran Haffenden (7)
**Kippax Ash Tree Primary School**

# My Garden

My garden is a special place,
An exciting place to be,
With nice tall trees
And beautiful flowers,
There's so much I can see.

In the pond we have leaping frogs,
They croak all day at me.
The butterflies flutter, the bees are busy,
Time for a cup of tea.

My trampoline is lots of fun,
And so is my new swing.
I like to play all day, all night,
It makes me want to sing.

Holly Doherty (8)
**Kippax Ash Tree Primary School**

# The Monsters

Some are ugly
Some are tall
Some are friendly
Some are small
Some are kind
Some are difficult to see
Some are in my family
Some are in my wardrobe at night
There are different possibilities.

Emma Birtwhistle (8)
**Kippax Ash Tree Primary School**

# Powers

If I had powers
I would fly around the world like a speedy aeroplane.

If I had powers
I would visit every single country in the world
To see all the exciting things they do.

If I had powers
I would race back in time like a time machine.

If I had powers
I would try to run as fast as lightning into the future
To see what's going to happen.

If I had powers
I would zoom to every planet in space like a huge rocket.

Kerry Richardson (10)
**Kippax Ash Tree Primary School**

# Fog

Creeping softly into the mysterious graveyard
Echoing down the scary wood as if it was unsuspected.

Laying silently through the alleyway like smoke
Has been born, hovering darkly onto the river.

Drooping slowly on the biggest lake in the UK
As if a star's falling slowly from the sky

Filling in every space in the woods and fields
People getting lost wherever they go.

Katie Sanderson (10)
**Kippax Ash Tree Primary School**

*Winner*

# Penguin

If I was a penguin
I would dive under the deep blue water
And try to catch some fish for my tea.

If I was a penguin
I would huddle in a massive group
As big as a herd of seals.

If I was a penguin
I would waddle away from the falling ice
As fast as I could.

If I was a penguin
I would dream of going to Asia
And walking the hot countries.

Rachael Birkenshaw (9)
**Kippax Ash Tree Primary School**

# Winter Comes Like . . .

Winter comes like a blanket drowning the Earth
Shivering children crawling along the grass
Silence every morning, nothing to hear and nothing to see.

Winter comes like birds flying to a small shelter
Slippery ice by the pond, slipping your way ice-skating
Whistling chicks by the barn
Mystical air and fog
Freezing bites in a fridge
Sprinkling sparkles everywhere and every day.

Nicole Watson (11)
**Kippax Ash Tree Primary School**

# Winter Like A Steam Train

Winter like a stream train trying to keep on tracks,
He fills the air with foggy smoke
And sounds like a distant foghorn.

Winter comes like a blanket of ice,
He slowly melts away till there is nothing left
But the pure green grass.

Winter comes like an ice cream,
He melts away, making the snow go
And the sun come.

Winter comes like a singing robin,
He flies through the sky,
And winter is coming today.

Russell Barton (10)
**Kippax Ash Tree Primary School**

# My Baby Brother

I've got a new baby brother.
'You've got to help look after him,' said my mother.
'Remember, he's a boy,
Not a toy.'
He cries when he does a poo,
But he doesn't go to the loo.
What can I do?
My mum says, 'Change his nappy,'
But I'm not happy!

Sufian Thompson (8)
**Kippax Ash Tree Primary School**

# Winter Like Snow

Winter like snow,
He knocks on everyone's windows
And tells us it's snow time.

Winter like a white tornado,
He throws himself around
And only leaves his white jacket behind.

Winter like a sheet of ice,
He is bumpy or smooth,
But absolutely freezing.

Winter like a sheep in summer,
His white fluffy coat comes off
And lays a white blanket.

James Byers (11)
**Kippax Ash Tree Primary School**

# Valentine

V is for Valentine cards that people give and receive
A is for adore the presents you get
L is for love in every letter
E is for enjoying the cards you are given
N is for nice food on
T he table
I is for irresistible things that you give me
N is for night-time, the time we all celebrate
E is for entertainment that we all love to see.

Maisie Louise Greer (8)
**Kippax Ash Tree Primary School**

# If I Had Four Legs

If I had four legs
I would be the fastest sprinter on the Earth's face.

If I had four legs
I would gallop across the shiny silver seas in search of treasure.

If I had four legs
I'd run all the marathons and win easy-peasy like Usain Bolt.

If I had four legs
I would attempt to break any record which includes sprinting.

If I had four leg
I would orbit the planets in exactly 22.2 seconds.

If I had four legs I would run, gallop, spring over and over again.

Jed Limbert (9)
**Kippax Ash Tree Primary School**

# Late

Got up this morning
Quilt puffed, 'Put me over you.'
'Can't' I said, 'late.'

Went downstairs
Remote clicked, 'Turn me over.'
'Can't,' I said, 'late.'

Got outside
Door creaked, 'Shut me.'
'Can't,' I said, 'late.'

Conor James Halkyard (10)
**Kippax Ash Tree Primary School**

# Funfair

Sun shining
Fluffy candyfloss
Puffy popcorn
Long queues
Spinning wheel
Creamy ice cream
Children screaming
Strawberry lollies
Fierce rides
Coaster lovers
Turning teacups
Long day
Home time.

Connor Walls (7)
**Kippax Ash Tree Primary School**

# Winter Like

Winter is like a high speed train,
Comes and leaves winter behind
And leaves a bed behind.

Winter is like a blanket of snow
Comes and puts autumn to bed
And waits for spring to come.

Winter is like a bed cover,
Comes like a person making a bed
And finally spring comes.

George Colledge (11)
**Kippax Ash Tree Primary School**

# Birthday Party

It's my best friend's party tomorrow
And I just can't wait
There'll be singing and dancing
I hope I'm not late.

I've got her a present
The best in the world
I'm wearing my pretty pink dress
And having my hair curled.

I can't wait to taste the cake
We already had a peek
Just then I remembered
It's not till next week.

Imogen Linley (8)
**Kippax Ash Tree Primary School**

# The Messenger from Hell

Last night I heard a fright,
I ran downstairs to see a sight.
A tall dark figure staring at me,
With its eyes like bumblebees.
It ran towards me at such a pace,
Then fear ran straight through my face.
It raised its big long arms to tell
That I was going straight to Hell.
Then suddenly the light switched on,
And I was in bed, all along.

Christopher Thorp (11)
**Kippax Ash Tree Primary School**

# Leah's Poem

Leah Flintoft goes to school
She may be 11 but she's no fool
She can dance and she can sing
In fact she can do almost any old thing
When Granny comes, she helps her cook
And doesn't need a recipe book.

She paints the pictures on the walls
Dances around and never falls
When Mum comes home she makes her tea
Mum's so pleased, we all can see
Dad's so tired after working late
I know he's here, I heard the gate.

Leah Flintoft (11)
**Kippax Ash Tree Primary School**

# The Gale

Extraordinary windy night
Gates parachuted off hinges
Lids exploded off rusty bins
Litter scattered everywhere.

Slates stripped from rooftops
Which smashed to the ground
Rustling leaves thrashed along the ground
As the wind scanned branches of extremely terrified trees
Wind, sounds like wolf howls
Near the glowing full moon.

Jenna Burns (11)
**Kippax Ash Tree Primary School**

# The Winter Like A Wolf

Winter like a wolf howling at midnight
Calling his fierce friends
Whilst he's eating a fox on a dinner table,
With snow and ice as plates and cups.

Winter like a tablecloth
Spreading through the towns and cities.
She is used to covering the mess
And taking autumn away.

Winter like a bullet train speeding up the world
So she can play on the tracks whilst carrying passengers,
Leaving the winter behind.

Ben Hardcastle (10)
**Kippax Ash Tree Primary School**

# Brimham Rocks

Today we went to Brimham Rocks,
We were wearing our thermal socks.
When I slipped on the icy path,
Me and my dad had a laugh.
When I went in the snow,
Off I went, here I go.
Faster and faster as I went,
I fell into the fence.
Oops, I made a dent.
Back to the car we went for a cup of tea,
Warmed my belly and home we did flee.

Lauren Obridge (11)
**Kippax Ash Tree Primary School**

# Planet

If I was a planet
I would be as cold as an ice cube.

If I was a planet
I would hear the sun shouting for help.

If I was a planet
I would feel my heart as freezing as the Arctic Circle.

If I was a planet
I would smell the rocket's ashes which it had left.

If I was a planet
I would see the stars as silver as tin foil.

Ayesha Goggs (9)
**Kippax Ash Tree Primary School**

# My Rabbit

Happy player,
Nose twitcher,
Dish tipper,
Soft fur,
Flower stealer,
Vegetable eater,
High hopper,
Small tail,
Hutch liver,
My friend.

Adam Hepworth (7)
**Kippax Ash Tree Primary School**

## Learning Logs

L earning logs are great
E veryone's different
A fabulous way to show what you have learnt
R eally fun
N o wrong answer
I t's better than a work sheet
N ever someone else's ideas
G reat for the teacher to mark

L ovely to work in
O nly supposed to do one or two pages
G o on, get one.

Natalie Sterland (10)
**Kippax Ash Tree Primary School**

## My Big Sister, Charlotte

My big sister, Charlotte, is smaller than me,
I lift her up quite easily.
She can't lift me, she's tried and tried,
I must have something heavy inside.
One night I lifted her up to bed,
I tucked her up with Tim, the ted.
I kissed her goodnight and went to my room,
I hoped Mum and Dad would be back soon.
I squeezed my teddy and fell asleep,
And slept and slept without a peep.

Emily Brown (11)
**Kippax Ash Tree Primary School**

## Snow Day

Snow, snow everywhere,
It's so cold, but I don't care.
Freezing fingers and freezing toes,
A cold face and a bright red nose
Snowball fights are really fun,
But be careful not to get hit by one.
As the snow is melting at the end of the day,
Inside the warm cosy house my mum shouts hooray.
What a fun day in the snow I've had,
When it's all gone by the morning, I will feel sad.

Leah Bootland (7)
**Kippax Ash Tree Primary School**

## Midnight Terror

I woke up in terror,
Gasping like a dog.
I could hear the wind howling,
As well as the fog.
Was it a dream,
Or was it all real?
But we'll never know
Because the creatures in my brain
They never go,
And leave me whining in pain.

Oliver Thompson (10)
**Kippax Ash Tree Primary School**

# The Woods

Dark gloomy trees creaking through cold mass of air
Squeaking rats running past narrow footpaths
Glowing moon spotted in the dusky dawn

Birds whistling through apple trees
Warm sun shining on muddy footpaths
Cooling air blowing gently on your face

Fog unravelling a thick layer
Mounting on trees
Branches snapping when your back is turned.

**Emily Lunn (10)**
**Kippax Ash Tree Primary School**

# Winter Like

Winter comes like a twinkling star
Covering the Earth with a white blanket
Cuddling up on the sofa.

Winter comes like candles burning
Fires warming freezing rooms
Angels singing relaxing tunes.

Winter comes like frosty icicles
She nips your feet and fingers
Walking across the crispy snow.

**Laura Georgia Wardell (11)**
**Kippax Ash Tree Primary School**

*Poetry Explorers – West Yorkshire*

# Christmas

C is for carols that people sing
H is for holly that hangs on your tree
R is for reindeer with noses glowing red
I is for icicles freezing cold
S is for snow falling down
T is for turkey steaming and hot
M is for mince pies tasty and nice
A is for Advent calendar with treats behind each door
S is for Santa bringing your presents.

Sarah O'Neill (8)
**Kippax Ash Tree Primary School**

# The Gale

Gale force winds pounding the treetops
Like a giant blowing the world to its misery
Flicking slates off the rooftops
Like a piece of dust, blowing the world to its misery
Trees thrashing about as the wind screams
Through the branches blowing the world to its misery
Wind whistling down the alleyway
Like a herd of elephants passing by
Blowing the world to its misery.

Jake Crossland (10)
**Kippax Ash Tree Primary School**

# The Snowman

The snow is falling all around,
Let's roll the snow on the ground,
We'll build a snowman, fat and round,
And wrap his scarf round and round.

We'll use a carrot for his nose
And some buttons for his coat.
Let's put a hat upon his head,
Then it's time to go to bed.

Rebecca Westerman (8)
**Kippax Ash Tree Primary School**

# 24 Hours In The Woods

Brightly coloured flowers dancing in the wind
Buzzing bees busily collecting pollen
Squirrels quickly gathering acorns, trying not to be seen
Morning dew glistening as the winter sun shines upon it.

Wind whistling your name through falling oak trees
Rotting branches suddenly fall as if from nowhere
Mist twisting, winding its way through overgrown trees
Amber eyes peering at you through the darkness.

Megan Laura Wright (11)
**Kippax Ash Tree Primary School**

# Snowball

S lowly, snow drops upon the slippery ground
N ow you can hear the snow pounding down
O utside is white and cold
W hile inside is warm and gold
B ut now we can go outside
A nd play and slip and slide
L ively children scream and shout
L ook, that's what it's all about.

Jessica Snaddon (7)
**Kippax Ash Tree Primary School**

# You Are My Angel

You are the one who looks over me,
You are my angel.
You are the one who could be cute as can be,
You are my angel.
You know what to do and when to see me,
You are my angel.
You are the brightest star at night,
You are my angel.

Libby Latto (10)
**Kippax Ash Tree Primary School**

# Holidays

H olidays are so much fun
O n the beach we can play all day
L azing about in the sun
I n the pool splashing away
D ancing at the disco
A fter tea we go and play some more
Y achting in the deep blue sea
S unny days are always fun.

Ellie Davis (8)
**Kippax Ash Tree Primary School**

# School Dinners

Standing in line with my tray,
About to be served my dinner.
The mashed potato is all lumpy,
The dinner ladies are extremely grumpy.
'Move along!' shout the dinner ladies.
'What do you want for pudding?'
I spy some jelly and runny ice cream.
I hate school dinners, I want to scream.

Ellie Doherty (8)
**Kippax Ash Tree Primary School**

# Friends

Some friends make you happy when you're feeling sad
I have lots of friends which makes me very glad.

Friends are like a smile inside your tummy
Some friends come to see if you want to play
And to check to see if you're OK.

My friends are helpful, nice and kind
Friends like these are hard to find.

Lauren Morley (8)
**Kippax Ash Tree Primary School**

# Chris W

C old is an illness as well as temperature and can be bad for some people
H ailstones are just like rocks falling from the sky
R ain is falling water just like a pond is in the sky
I ce is rock solid and could break glass
S now is crystal white as it has just been painted

W inter is a cold time where people can get cold.

Christopher Winter (10)
**Kippax Ash Tree Primary School**

## The Rock Band Poem

If I was in a band
I would rock all night underneath the moonlight
Singing as loud as a lion roaring
I'd hear the crowd cheer and scream
And it makes me feel I'm the king of the bass
If I was in a band I would play
Every Aerosmith song in the world.

Joshua Whaley (10)
**Kippax Ash Tree Primary School**

## Snowman

S ledding is lots of fun
N oses are red and glowing
O pen fires roaring
W hite, bright and fluffy snow
M aking snowballs to throw
A ll the children playing
N ice cold snow melts in your hand.

Kieron England (8)
**Kippax Ash Tree Primary School**

# Fog!

Scaring everyone, the bright thick fog comes rolling in
Mysteriously it squeezes through the fences, splitting up and
rejoining at the end
Creeping through the ghostly graveyard as people rest in peace
Cracked blocks on the floor from ancient graves
Stalking like a ghost, down the creepy alleyway
As it looks like it never stops.

Callum Grainger (10)
**Kippax Ash Tree Primary School**

# Fluffy

My hamster's name is Fluffy
She is small, white and cuddly
She sleeps in the day and plays through the night
The noise of her play wheel gives me such a fright
And when she's tired out I am wide awake and want to play
But Fluffy's content to sleep the day away.

Jasmin Cartwright (7)
**Kippax Ash Tree Primary School**

# Baking

Baking is so much fun
I often bake with my mum
I like to make biscuits and cakes
The best bit is when they are made
Then I can ice them and eat them all up
But the worst part is the washing up.

**Georgia Cattle (9)**
**Kippax Ash Tree Primary School**

# Fog

Disguising itself across the never-ending field
Creeping up on you whilst you're asleep
Floating scarily through a mysterious graveyard
Freezing old-age pensioners cruelly in an ancient garden
Hovering silently through scary gardens
Flying fluently through dark skies.

**Sam Ward (11)**
**Kippax Ash Tree Primary School**

# Chocolate

If the world was covered in chocolate
I would eat all of it
If there was a hot chocolate stream
I would bath in it and drink all of it
If the world was cookies, choc-chip, white
I'd pray to God.

Aaron Booth (9)
**Kippax Ash Tree Primary School**

# Sharks

Shell-breaker
Coral-wrecker
Fish-eater
Boat-smasher
People-trapper
Tail-swisher.

Sam Lunn (7)
**Kippax Ash Tree Primary School**

# Brimham Rocks

At the weekend we did go to Brimham Rocks to play in the snow
As Dad pulled me up the path, it was so much fun it made me laugh
Mum pulled me into the heather, into the snow we went all together
Mum pushed me down the hill, faster and faster, what a thrill
Back to the car to get dry, time to go home, we must fly.

Hannah Obridge (8)
**Kippax Ash Tree Primary School**

# Billy

B illy is my pet parrot
I n his cage he lives
L ong and loud is his laughter
L oveable and cute sitting on his perch
Y et watch out, he may bite.

### Nathan Newton (7)
**Kippax Ash Tree Primary School**

# Lights

Lights are like stars put together
Lights are like silver paint on a big black canvas
Lights are like silver fireworks in the dark sky
Lights are like silver trees in the black sky
Lights are like silver chalk on a black carpet.

### Corrine Perkins (8)
**Kippax Ash Tree Primary School**

# Rugby

R unning hard and straight
U p the touchline pushing on
G oing for the try-line
B all in my hand, running strong
Y es, I've scored a try, my team is singing the winner's song.

### Charlotte Byers (7)
**Kippax Ash Tree Primary School**

## Pantomimes

Imagination, laughter,
Booing, screaming, cheering,
Full of fun and full of colour,
Clapping, singing, dancing,
Noisy characters.

Harry Goodall (7)
**Kippax Ash Tree Primary School**

## Army

A collection of guns
R ed blood on the ground
M en charging at the enemy
Y elling when they charge.

James Saxon (7)
**Kippax Ash Tree Primary School**

## The Fire-Breathing Monster

D ragons, dark, evil and fiery
R oars as loud as thunder
A good dragon is a rare sight
G old, silver, bronze, the dragon guards
O range fire flies from its mouth
N o one has ever seen a dragon fly.

Henry Milner (10)
**Methodist J&I School**

# Transport

The years of steam trains passing by
Trains built long ago
The Flying Scotsman, The Mallard
We no longer see
Their destiny is now a museum.

Journey through time and travel
The mighty Subaru, sleek and fast
Boasting to other cars
With its loud twin exhausts
Be aware Subaru drivers
Speed police, speed police
Flashing lights, soaring sirens.

Getting even faster
The sound barrier is broken
Concorde engines zooming by
Silently and sweet
Like a flying unicorn
Gliding through the sky
Oh, what a sight.

When will it ever end?
Will it drive us round the bend?

Joseph Morris (10)
**Methodist J&I School**

# In The Jungle

In the jungle the lion snores
Then wakes up and stretches his claws
He pounces with a mighty roar
And bashes a zebra to the floor.

In the jungle a monkey sleeps
When he wakes he eats and eats
Then up a tree he climbs
And swings on all the long thin vines.

In the jungle a giraffe stands tall
Watching the cheetahs thinking they're cool
The giraffe towers up so high
That she can see the birds in the sky.

In the jungle the hippo is fat
She rolls in the mud, it's as simple as that
She walks proud with her young
Then stops at a waterhole to have some fun.

The jungle is wonderful and very nice
With creatures from lions to little mice
The lakes are beautiful and so are the trees
But the noise is horrendous, so be quiet please!

Sam Winder (10)
**Methodist J&I School**

# Hiding In The Coral

H ermit crabs hiding down
I n the rocks they are found
D olphins leaping up above
I n the coral that I love
N early everything that you can see
G orgeous fish hiding in anemones.

I t's the sea cucumbers that get me
N ow I'm scared of the eels with their zap!

T errifying sharks with their big sharp teeth
H ow many things are there in the reef?
E normous whales always moaning

C lown fish swimming round and playing
O ctopus with eight squirty legs
R aging oceans rocking seabeds
A ngelfish swimming gracefully
L obsters clawing at their prey.

That's what the reef is all about.

Jayne Davidson-Page (10)
**Methodist J&I School**

# Mammoths – Haiku

Stomp, stomp, here they are
Mammoths raging through the Earth
Great trunks we can see.

Hannah Davidson-Page (10)
**Methodist J&I School**

## World Of Pollution

Litter in the park
Litter down the drain
Killing helpless larks
And that's just insane.

Down the roads
In the street
Killing toads
And destroying wheat.

Trucks and lorries choke the ozone
We really, really need to worry
It's not too late to say we're sorry
So leave the atmosphere alone.

So trash your cars
And buy a bike
Then we can carry on seeing the stars
And the light if you like.

Michael Willis (10)
**Methodist J&I School**

## Clouds

Clouds, clouds everywhere
How many things can you see from up there?
Are you slimy? Are you soft?
Have you ever been put in a loft?
I think you're fluffy or are you not? You look puffy
I think that's true, I wish I could come up there and see you.

Grace Byrom (7)
**Methodist J&I School**

# The Cat That Made The World

The little cat asleep in bed
The cat that made the world
His little head on his tiny paw
Dreaming dreams so soft and safe.

First of all he wanted land
So he mushed up all of the clouds
But it all looked very bland
The little cat needed some help.

He called all his little friends
All forty came at once
They all were thirsty, needed water
They cried and cried to make some sea.

The little cat just woke up
The little cat is now awake
Happy now, awake today
A dream is a dream, keep it safe.

Amy Winder (10)
**Methodist J&I School**

# Space

S tars twinkle at night
P lanets spinning around and around
A liens life forms real or not?
C ircling planets orbit the Earth
E normous meteors gathering speed.

Matthew Greener (10)
**Methodist J&I School**

# Down Deep In The Sea

Down deep in the sea
Fish will swim round you and me
Rocky caves we will see
Down deep in the sea.

Down deep in the sea
Swimming turtles we will see
Hiding amongst they'll be
Down deep in the sea.

Down deep in the sea
Shipwrecks we will see
Covered in sea salt they will be
Down deep in the sea.

Down deep in the sea
Around coral reef divers see
All the fish patterned beautifully
Down deep in the sea.

Lucy Cooper (10)
**Methodist J&I School**

# Clouds

As cool as a cucumber
A rain cloud, storm cloud, crack goes the lightning cloud
*Boom*, a thundercloud is angry
Calm cloud as fluffy as a poodle, as still as the sea
There's a cloud up there looking down on me.

Olivia Marsh (8)
**Methodist J&I School**

# A Hike To Where?

Jogging, running, skipping, hopping
They're some sports I like
Netball, football, basketball, skiball
But sometimes I fancy a hike.

But a hike to where?
Where to start? Where to end?
Maybe in town to look in some shops
But if so, I'd take some money to spend.

I guess that's not what you'd call a hike
A hike's usually by hills or countryside
If it takes too long stay in a tent
Now how to put it up, I wish I had a guide.

And now I'm at home, laying on my bed
Staring outside to see what I can see
A camera crew, actors, just where I have been
And now I've just realised I could have been on TV.

Antonia Stephenson (10)
**Methodist J&I School**

## The Jungle

The lions sleep
When the rain is deep
The monkeys swing
But the birds love to sing.

The tiger gives a big roar
When something stabs it in the paw
The deer does a big run
When it hears the bang of a gun!

In the jungle
There is a bundle
Of animals
But no camels.

Thomas Wolfe (10)
**Methodist J&I School**

## Space Out

Black holes
Rocket ships
Adventurous astronauts
Weird Martians
Bright stars
Shooting meteors
Invisible UFO
Changing moon
Colossal craters
*Space!*

Ellis Abbott (10)
**Methodist J&I School**

# The Rainforest

The swinging monkey
He eats and eats
The dancing monkey
Who taps his feet.

The tough tiger
Sharpens his claws
The clever tiger
Roars and roars.

In the rainforest it's very wet
The plants grow and grow
Humans come and get a sweat
And glow-worms glow and glow.

Elizabeth Arnott (10)
**Methodist J&I School**

# A Mythical Creature

Flies high in the sky
Healing injured creatures
Feathered and hot
Turns to ash when it dies
A beak with human-sized nostrils.

Red and orange feathers, blazing with heat
In the volcano she will sleep
A tongue the wingspan of an eagle
She is a magnificent phoenix.

Joe Callaghan (10)
**Methodist J&I School**

# In The Jungle

A monkey is swinging through the trees
Below is a rhino with knobbly knees
There is a lion with a mane rather shaggy
And an elephant with skin quite baggy.

In a tree sits a snake with a fork-shaped tongue
And look at that panther protecting its young
In the distance is a zebra with stripes, white and black
Look out for any tigers that can't wait to attack.

While parrots squawk high above our heads
Mother cheetahs put their babies to their beds
A spider spins a web of silky thread
There's a crowd of hyenas laughing ahead.

Marie Aylward (11)
**Methodist J&I School**

# Hunted

Down in the jungle where nobody goes
There was a bundle that nobody knows.

There was a bang, creeping about there was a man
Hunting about as fast as he could, whilst all the birds sang.

The lions roared, the snakes slithered
Across the floor, the elephant dithered.

The monkey chirped, the jaguar ran
The lion hurt the gunman.

Seth Jackson (10)
**Methodist J&I School**

# What I Saw

In space I saw a big spaceship
Hiding in the stars
It was flying high, but took a dip
And ended up on Mars.

In space I saw some red eyes
Staring hard at me
It was an alien and his spies
So I thought I'd better flee.

In space I saw some glowing green slime
I scooped it up and my hand turned green
But the glowing had gone and it looked like grime
So I thought I'd use some Mr Sheen.

Daniel Thompson (9)
**Methodist J&I School**

# Flower

Petals cute, roots grow, pretty white rose
Need water and sunlight to offer you the rose
Stem with leaves with thorns
Flower pink or red or white
Seeds little as a bee
Small and dirty, love your look
Smooth flower, cute as me
Like a summer that's hot as me
Smell nice, soft as skin.

Abbey Matthews (7)
**Methodist J&I School**

# In The Dark Moonlit Sky

In the dark moonlit sky
The bright stars twinkling
The Earth is spinning round and round
With a slow gentle flow.

In the dark moonlit sky
Sat a silvery glistening moon
Rockets shooting up high
With their burning bright fire.

In the dark moonlit sky
Astronauts searching for clues
A flashing rainbow-coloured comet
Disappearing on its journey of the galaxy.

Victoria Truelove (9)
**Methodist J&I School**

# Space

S paceships are flying round space
P eace in space, no noise at all
A ll the stars floating through space
C rater, the giant hole
E normous meteors flying through space
S pace is silent
H oles all over the moon
I n space there are colours all over
P lanets big and round.

Ben Ascough (9)
**Methodist J&I School**

# Jungle

Monkeys, monkeys everywhere
Parrots flying in the air
Spiders, snakes and chimpanzees
Butterflies float in the breeze
Tigers roar everywhere
Don't look now, you'll get scared.

Animals, animals everywhere
Birds are flying in the air
Ants, sloths and geckos
Listen to the different echoes
Animals, animals everywhere
I would like to go, but will I dare?

Ismael Ajaz (11)
**Methodist J&I School**

# Flower

Tall, tall flower as tall as a giraffe
As scented as a perfume bottle

As beautiful as a rose
As cool as me and attractive as me
And beautiful and colourful.

You're as pretty as me
A butterfly on you taking the nectar on or off
Pretty and blue, I love to smell you.

Emily Pittam (8)
**Methodist J&I School**

# The Sea

The sea's waves
Overflowing the caves
The sea's fish
Being sold in a dish.

The humans in the sea making a splash
Hitting the rocks it sounds like a crash
Oh no, there's a whirlpool ahead
All the fish and animals are going to be *dead!*

But the fish and sharks are swimming away
Now everything will be okay.

Sam Thompson (9)
**Methodist J&I School**

# In The Sea

In the sea there are many creatures
Most of them have a lot of interesting features
At the top of the sea there are many boats
Little fish wondering what they are whilst wearing their coats.

In the sea you can find whales
A lot of them have long tails
At the bottom of the sea you can find treasure
People who do find it a pleasure.

Alishah Arshid (10)
**Methodist J&I School**

# Shark Attack

Seas are soothing, calm and quiet
But when the shark comes, there's a riot
So all the fish run away
Just like they did yesterday.

So don't be fooled by the rippling tide
Because when a shark comes, we all hide
All the dangers in the sea
Are waiting to eat you and me.

Megan Ball (10)
**Methodist J&I School**

# Time Travel

Time
Travelling back
Off I go with a flash
Through the porthole of time
I'm travelling back, where
Will I go, what era?
I hope it's not the dinosaurs
*Roar!*

Nathan Hinley (10)
**Methodist J&I School**

# Animals

A lligators snapping their jaws
N ewts flicking their long tails
I guanas warming up in the sun
M onkeys climbing up the trees
A nts running about in the grass
L eopards running as fast as the wind
S nakes slithering on the ground.

Owen Addy (10)
**Methodist J&I School**

# In Space

Space
Peaceful place
Aliens in spaceships
Silver moon, stars shining
In the sky
Spaceships moving
Everywhere!

Aqeel Ajaz (9)
**Methodist J&I School**

## The Hydra

Hydra
Bloodthirsty
Big, scaly, scary
Growling, stomping, angrily, fiercely
Breathing out steam
The Hydra
Deadly.

**Samuel Atkinson (11)**
**Methodist J&I School**

## Time Travel

Where shall I go, future of past?
The time machine will travel at the speed of light
And maybe give you a bumpy flight
To get to my destination at last.

Back to when the dinosaurs ruled
Some like cute, but don't be fooled
Lots of different, strange kinds
And if you are quiet you may hear pterodactyls whines.

Way in the future now
When Earth is in trouble
Martians kill humans
And put mind control on cows.

Now back to when I lived
If you liked it just say
Then I'll be sure to take you to those places
One day.

**Lucas John Blackwell (10)**
**Methodist J&I School**

Poetry Explorers – West Yorkshire

# The Swordfish

Swimming with the shoals of fish
That surround the reefs of time
Swimming with the dark grey rocks
Which reflect the times gone by
Then, a worm in front of him
The bait, the line, the hook.

But now he's swimming in Reef Aquarium
A tank the size of a man
Swimming through the unclean water
Watching passers-by
He's watching from a corner
Watching, watching, waiting.

Now he's swimming through a dark, grey, sea cave
An anxious cod circles him
He's swimming to a bright white light
Everlasting, ever taunting
Then he wakes, he was dreaming
Ever thinking, ever dreaming, ever hoping.

Now he's back, but wait,
Something's wrong
What happened to the clear blue waters?
What happened to the shoals of fish
Glittering with bright silver scales?
What happened to the reefs of dark grey rock?
What happened to the land he used to know?

Django Claughan (9)
**Old Town Primary School**

# A Lifetime Ago

Freezing grey concrete
Surrounding wire mesh
Desolate buildings
Something is there
Shaking with cold
Blank-eyed
Half remembering
A lifetime ago . . .

He sees an elephant
Warm brown eyes
He sees a water hole
Calves splashing happily
But then he's back
In a cold, dark zoo
Half remembering
A lifetime ago . . .

Litter strewn
Along a path
Hard, dry ground
A single car passes
Headlights flash his way
He looks but turns away
Half remembering
A lifetime ago . . .

Katy Blagg (11)
**Old Town Primary School**

# The Leopard

Feeling imprisoned
Laying in the cold wet straw
Exposed to the public
Wishing, hoping, dreaming
Of the place that lies beyond.

Once he was purring
In the dense bush then
He looks, listens, sniffs
A vehicle, a man, a gun
Then nothing
He wakes up dizzy
Where is he?
A zoo.

Now he's trapped
In a zoo where
The public is the only view
One glance left -
One glance right -
Humans, he hates
That sight.

Joe Law (10)
**Old Town Primary School**

# Caged Tiger

Burning eyes
Sleek, striped coat
A deep dark rumble
Emanates from his throat
He paces back, he paces forth
To the south and to the north.

Sleeping still
He's had his fill
Of tender meat
And of the heat.

Dimming eyes
Rough, striped coat
A soft, quiet rumble
Emanates from his throat
He paces back, he paces forth
To the south and to the north.

Lugh Martin (10)
**Old Town Primary School**

# The Lion

*Pat, pat, pat*
My cold paws step on the hard concrete floor
I look out to amazed faces through cold wire meshing
They're scared . . .
But I'm even more scared.

My dad drags back food
Hyenas try to steal it
We hear a shot of a gun . . .
I run
We run
They've got me.

And now I'm here
My cold paws step on the hard concrete floor
I look out to . . .
A dark, empty corridor.

Molly Stansfield (10)
**Old Town Primary School**

# Volcanoes

Volcanoes are very strong
They can be anywhere
Volcanoes erupt before your eyes
Volcanoes' lava is not hot, it's boiling
When volcanoes erupt, they are as loud as thunder
Volcanoes can make lots of rock fly.

Josh Mitchell (7)
**Primrose Lane Primary School**

# Colours

Red is like burning fire as hot as the sun
It may look nice but it isn't fun
Yellow daffodils as beautiful as gems
Easter is coming, we need eggs from the hens
Green is as fresh as the grass
We have some near our class
Blue looks as cold as ice
The polar bears look cuddly
But aren't really that nice
Black is as dark as the night sky
If you listen carefully
You'll hear the owls pass by.

Rachel Duxbury (8)
**Primrose Lane Primary School**

# What Am I?

What am I?
I sizzle and sparkle
I shine in the fiery sun
I make good things happen
I make punishments.

I'm as colourful as a rainbow
I work for a wizard
I am not a person
I glimmer like silver in the sun.

A: Magic!

Alicia Batley (8)
**Primrose Lane Primary School**

# Volcanoes

Red and
Orange explosions
From the ground
Big, black, thick smoke
Floating to the sky
If I were there it would be very
Magnificent. Boiling hot fire kills if you touch
As hot as the sun, fiery hot, ouch!
As wet as slime, wet and gooey
As tall as a tree
Seems to be growing up with me!

Jemima Browning (8)
**Primrose Lane Primary School**

# Puppies

Puppies are cheeky
Puppies are loud
They're as fast as a sports car
And they always make you proud
They're as bouncy as a ball
Adorable and fast
And when it's a race
They're never last
If you are sad they fill you with glee
And they always try their best to make you happy.

Lucy Toogood (7)
**Primrose Lane Primary School**

# Football

A football is as round as a ball
It rolls like thunder
Is hurt every day
And it's spotty, black and white
It gets kicked, so it is brave.

**Ryan Lawn (8)**
**Primrose Lane Primary School**

# Flowers

A flower is a lovely thing in spring
Yellow and red and purple and white like disco lights
Flowers make you feel happy and bright
Full of nature you can tell by the smell
Flowers are as colourful as a rainbow.

**Sarah Kirsty Halliday (8)**
**Primrose Lane Primary School**

# Lion

A grumpy brute lolloping through the jungle
Roaring as loud as a foghorn
It crunches its prey with its powerful fangs
Leaping as high as Heaven
A lion's mane is as precious as gold.

**Joseph Thomson (7)**
**Primrose Lane Primary School**

# Volcano

Deep inside the belly of the volcano
Bubbling, fiery, hot lava rising higher and higher
As time is flying by
Lava exploding deep inside
Shooting into the sky. *Boom!*

Ben Spink (7)
**Primrose Lane Primary School**

# Snail

Curling, curling round and round
Like wool that has been wound
Slithering slowly across the ground
All that is left is a slimy silver trail
And that is the mark of a snail.

Lily Dell (7)
**Primrose Lane Primary School**

# Computers

Computers are fun
You can play lots of games
Computers are intelligent
Computers are bright.

Tom Hepworth (7)
**Primrose Lane Primary School**

# Lions

Lions are like big cats
Lions roar like thunder
Lions are as scary as a horror film
Lions are as fast as lightning.

James Cahill (7)
**Primrose Lane Primary School**

# Light Blue Dolphin

I am a light blue dolphin
I live in the sea
I think it is cool and very nice
And I make sounds like *eek*.

Sometimes I swim slow
And sometimes very fast
I drink seawater
And sometimes I eat seaweed.

I can jump through hoops
I think it's very nice
I am smooth and soft
And maybe I am strong.

Jasmine Simmons (7)
**Richmond Hill Primary School**

# Cat

I'm a big fat cat
I live in a house
I love to lick milk
And to race about
I like to eat fish
But I hate water.

Alexander Tepsic (7)
**Richmond Hill Primary School**

# I Am A Fish

I'm a fish with fins and gills
I live in the sea of ocean blue
I like to eat seaweed and plankton too
And I swim faster than you.

Joe Daniels (7)
**Richmond Hill Primary School**

# Gold And Yellow Fish

I am a gold and yellow fish
I live in the sea
I eat seaweed
And I like to be free.

Ethan Wormald (8)
**Richmond Hill Primary School**

# Glimmering Swirls

Glittering lines
Glimmering swirls
Colourful walls
Beautiful rainbows
Gorgeous colours
Glorious gold
Sparkling curls
Bright light
Fabulous flowers
Shining sea blue
Refreshing green
Fiery orange.

Charlotte Rimmington (7)
**Towngate Primary School**

# The Golden Planet

Running and jumping on a gold planet
Dancing and prancing on golden leaves
Feeling like I'm in Heaven
Bars of glimmering gold
Colours run and dash
Curl and twirl
Suddenly a ray of gold dazzles the sky
Unexpectedly a bolt of fiery yellow
Shooting across the sky
Then, silence!

Matthew Wilson (8)
**Towngate Primary School**

# A Frosty Icicle

Upside down shimmering icicles
A river of sparkles
A tree that Jack Frost has frozen
A cloud made of ice
A glowing crystal at the bottom of a tree
A ball of snowy ice
A sparkling star shaped like a tree
Skating on ice
See-through glitter
Branch of a tree
A raindrop of ice.

Amy Charlotte Pickering (7)
**Towngate Primary School**

# Dreadful Germs!

A lonely and deadly place
Murky colours
Creak as you walk
Particles of diamonds
Spectacular crystal effect
Unusual shapes
Light and dark shades
Immaculate background.

Sophie Kay Jarman (8)
**Towngate Primary School**

# The Crystal Poem

Like walking in a colourful volcano
Ice crystals all over the place
Beautiful colours all around us
Spectacular multicolours
Glimmering glitter
Golden glitter
Shining in your eyes.

Molly Walker (7)
**Towngate Primary School**

# The Icy Maze

Walking through the icy maze
Feeling I have to run
The icy maze
Starts to get darker
I feel I need to run faster
Spikes come out of the ice
I'm stuck, trying to get through the icy maze.

Harry Revell-Jackson (8)
**Towngate Primary School**

# Untitled

Walking down a crystal corridor, seeing light ahead
Lots of colours around you, every step you hear a tinkle
Hear strange sounds, know you're very safe
Every crystal always shiny
Odd patterns on the wall, footprints on the floor
Shattered windows fixed with crystal.

Zach Fletcher (7)
**Towngate Primary School**

# Magical World Of Rocks

Gold, glimmering, glitter
Blue sparkling pebbles on the snow
Freezing cold, shining snow
Pebbles under the snow
Dark blue sky.

Ruth Sterry (7)
**Towngate Primary School**

# Sparkling Diamonds

Shining star
Green glass
Sharp teeth as sharp as can be
Green water that is frozen
Shimmering diamonds on the sandy beach.

Nathan Brummitt (7)
**Towngate Primary School**

# City Buildings Tower Over Me

Sitting on a bench
I can see litter scattered in every direction

Gleaming taxis slide down hills
Long bridges rock in the wind
Washing on balconies flaps like elephants' ears

Rain sieves the city
Freezing air slams against my face
Crowds push past like brushes

Street traders shout in the wind
Police sirens scream in my ears
Motorbikes grumble like hungry lions

Fish markets are magnets for stray cats
Exhaust fumes pollute the environment
The smell of dustbins chokes me

Sitting on a bench
City buildings tower over me.

Emma Street (10)
**Wellington Primary School**

# The Germans

They dropped bombs down on me
Big searchlights gleaming up at them
Innocent people getting hurt
The machine guns aiming right at me
As the Germans bombed London!

Joe Newell (9)
**Wellington Primary School**

# Air Raid

I was sitting in the kitchen
With my mum and dad
When the siren wailed
It was very, very bad.

Running in the shelter
Very, very afraid
The aeroplanes were coming
With another air raid.

Sitting in the shelter
Singing a silly song
Hoping that the planes
Wouldn't stay very long.

All is quiet
So we head to the door
Back to our house
Safe once more.

Megan Spence-Hill (9)
**Wellington Primary School**

# Space

S pace is all around
P lanets moving fast
A ll planets are spinning
C omets zooming round
E arth, our home planet.

Dominic Burdett (9)
**Wellington Primary School**

# The Trenches

In the trenches there were guns
Loaded, ready to fire killer bullets.

Sandbags ready to protect
In front, behind and to the side
Rock-hard helmets on their heads
Loose straps under their chins.

These soldiers were unwashed
Waiting for unleashed reinforcements
Long hours watching throughout the night
Waiting calmly for the enemy.

Enemy approaches silently
Stopped by sharp barbed wire
Coiled in circles
Glinting in the moonlight
No other light in sight.

Samir Cradock (8)
**Wellington Primary School**

## School And Teachers

S pellings are important
C hildren have fun and learn
H elping others is really kind
O utstanding work is worth one point
O utside in the playground
L unch is at quarter-past twelve!

And

T eachers are amazing
E xciting education
A ssemblies are interesting
C lassrooms are a place of learning
H andwriting practise is always going on
E xperiments in science
R eading on Wise Owl (the highest level)
S cience is so great!

Hannah Scowby (8)
**Wellington Primary School**

## Dinosaurs

Dinosaurs, big or small
Charge fast or slow
Vicious beasts
King of the ginormous jungle
The boss of all animals
But they're all dead
So you won't see one again.

Morgan Dawson (8)
**Wellington Primary School**

# Small And Lonely In The Busy City

Leaning on a lamp post
I can see crowds of people passing by.

Litter blows lifeless across the streets
The homeless desperately beg shoppers for money
Cars race like cheetahs after prey.

Heat from the tarmac burns my feet
Refreshing rain falls on upturned faces
Cold stone statues stand to attention.

Police sirens scream on their way to emergencies
Brakes squeal as taxis stop reluctantly
Motorbikes rev like lions growling.

Leaning on a lamp post
I feel small and lonely in the busy city.

Nick Jasper (10)
**Wellington Primary School**

# Witch, Witch

Witch, witch, way up high
Witch, witch, I see you in the sky
Witch, witch, where do you eat?
Witch, witch, eats in evil street
Witch, witch, what do you drink?
Witch, witch, drinks dead frogs' ink
Witch, witch, where do you sleep?
Witch, witch, sleeps in her lair in a heap.

Ashleigh Yates (8)
**Wellington Primary School**

# Towering Over Me

Standing outside a shop
I can see graffiti scrawled everywhere.

Desperate beggars are ignored by passers-by
Robotic lights flash repeatedly
Shiny bright cars slither along.

Snow falls on my cold face
Wet clammy fog blocks my view
My feet shiver in the freezing weather.

Police sirens wail loudly
Gutters guzzle down water
Motorbikes roar past me.

Standing outside a shop
I feel tiny with skyscrapers towering over me.

Asim Ali (10)
**Wellington Primary School**

# My Dog

Tail wagger
Noisy barker
Cat chaser
Strong fighter
High jumper
Food eater
Hard biter
A good friend.

Rahim Rashid (9)
**Wellington Primary School**

# Frightened And Alone In The City

Sitting at a street cafe
I can see cars snaking in hundreds of directions

Street lamps gleam in the moonlight
Homeless people plead for coins
Crowds chat like monkeys in a zoo

Heat from cars surround me
Wet clammy fog claws at my face
Mist dances about like snow

Church bells scream in my ears
Sirens wail as they speed past
Motorbikes grumble like cheetahs on the run

Sitting at a street cafe
I feel frightened and alone.

Jessica Barron (10)
**Wellington Primary School**

# Lonely And Scared In The City

Standing in a shop doorway
I can see hundreds of people crushing others

The homeless sit alone on the cold pavements
Shop doors open and close constantly
Cars swamp the motorway like an army of ants

Desperate shoppers push past
I sink into the scorching hot tarmac
Humidity drenches me like warm rain

Train whistles deafen you when they scream
Buskers play tirelessly
Feet march on like soldiers on parade

Standing in a shop doorway
I feel lonely and scared.

Adam Frost (10)
**Wellington Primary School**

# Cramped In The City

Sitting outside a cafe
I can see litter scattered everywhere

Neon lights flash on and off
Skyscrapers tower tall over me
Shoppers charge into shops like cheetahs

Fog clouds my wet face
Heat from the tarmac burns my feet
Rain is like a shower as water splashes on my face

Sirens wail and deafen passers-by
Buskers play energetically hoping for money
Crowds are busy like bees in a hive

Sitting outside a cafe
I can see litter scattered everywhere.

Aaron Kundi (10)
**Wellington Primary School**

## Enslaved By The City

Standing at the top of a building
I can see millions of people walking by

Cars drive past in polluted fog
Dumped newspapers burn in dustbins
Motorbikes prowl round the streets

Rushing crowds brush against me
Rain sprays my face with water droplets
Heat slithers out from shop windows

Street traders yell out their wares
Trains whistle impatiently
Voices drown out buildings

Standing at the top of a building
I feel enslaved by the city.

Nathanial Rhodes (11)
**Wellington Primary School**

# Drowned By The Activity Of The City

Sitting on a bench
I can see the whole city in front of me.

Cold metal cars roll along
Bicycles stop suddenly at traffic lights
Jet-black motorways snake through the city.

Sharp wind claws my cold body
Rain covers the city in a grey cloud
Wet stones shiver underneath my feet.

Traffic purrs through streets
Motorbikes grumble as they weave through cars
Sirens wail like seagulls overhead.

Sitting on a bench
I feel drowned by the activity of the city.

Nathan Crane (10)
**Wellington Primary School**

# A Twisted Dream In The City

Standing in front of a busy shop
I can see crowds of people jostling each other

Beggars plead for hope from pedestrians
Gloomy trees watch my every move
Blue cameras flash like torches

Clammy fog surrounds me
Heat rises up from the pavements
A welcome breeze tickles my cheeks

Police sirens wail
Angry taxis blow their horns
Brakes squeal like injured cats

Standing in front of a busy shop
I feel I'm in a twisted dream.

David Stainsby (11)
**Wellington Primary School**

# WWII

In 1939 there was a fight
Around the world there were some nasty sights
Lots of men and ladies had to leave home
But some lucky ones stayed at home with children.

Everybody had different jobs to do
Some made planes and flew them too
Lots of ladies became nurses
Looking after all the injured cases.

In 1945 the fighting stopped
All the ladies and men went home
They welcomed the sight of the family home
But the saddest thing, some didn't make it home.

James Smith (8)
**Wellington Primary School**

# Friendship

F riends are good to have
R emember to be good and kind
I f we are upset our friends can make it better
E veryone that you meet, remember to be kind
N ice people are always the best
D on't get mad or angry at the people that you like
S hare our toys and the things we like
H appy friends makes me happy
I nvite them all to our parties
P arties are the best only with friends.

Keiran Child (8)
**Wellington Primary School**

*Poetry Explorers – West Yorkshire*

# Frederic And Mimi

On top of a hill in a cold shabby house
Lived a small brown creature called Mimi the mouse
In the same building with old Grandpa Nat
Was a much bigger creature, Frederic the cat.

This cat was a bully, awful and mean
And normally sleeping as Mimi had seen
But when he awoke and got up from the floor
All the mice hid and shut their small doors.

One day Frederic was taken for he had dome something bad
And poor Grandpa Nat was terribly sad
All the mice celebrated for the cat wasn't here
And Mimi the mouse giggled and gave a great cheer.

Rosie Shackleton (10)
**Wellington Primary School**

# Friendship

My friends are very special
They make me smile and cheer

Friends are people we know very well
We share and care and help each other

In the playground we run around
Playing lots of playground games

A friend is someone who can make me smile
Laugh and giggle for a while.

Thomas Rushworth (8)
**Wellington Primary School**

# I Like...

I like the colour red
It reminds me of my warm cosy bed
I like the colour green
I think it looks squeaky clean
I like the colour pink
It makes me clever and makes me think
I like the colour blue
It makes me think just of you
I like the colour black
Because it's the same as Santa's sack
This poem I'm sure I'll keep
But now it's time to go to sleep.

Alicia Blum (10)
**Wellington Primary School**

# My Hamster

Long whiskers
Bright eyes
Sharp teeth
Tiny feet
Fluffy fur
Pink nose
Peanut eater
Full cheeks
Fast roller
Good escaper
Hand biter
She's my best friend.

Lucy Tattersfield (7)
**Wellington Primary School**

Poetry Explorers – West Yorkshire

# My Cat

Mouse killer
Cotton player
People scratcher
Dog hater
Seat stealer
Food nicker
Self cleaner
Snow hater
People lover
Bird stalker
Vole hunter
A fluffy friend.

Rebecca Elyse Riley (9)
**Wellington Primary School**

# Young Writers Information

We hope you have enjoyed reading this book - and that you will continue to enjoy it in the coming years.

If you like reading and writing poetry drop us a line, or give us a call, and we'll send you a free information pack.

Alternatively if you would like to order further copies of this book or any of our other titles, then please give us a call or log onto our website at www.youngwriters.co.uk

Young Writers Information
Remus House
Coltsfoot Drive
Peterborough
PE2 9JX
(01733) 890066